CHANGING GEARS

THE EXPERIENCES AND OBSERVATIONS OF A
RETIRED STATE INVESTIGATOR TURNED ROOKIE TRUCK DRIVER

CHRISTOPHER O'HANLON

iUniverse LLC
Bloomington

CHANGING GEARS
The Experiences and Observations of a Retired State
Investigator Turned Rookie Truck Driver

iUniverse books may be ordered through booksellers or by contacting:

iUniverse LLC
1663 Liberty Drive
Bloomington, IN 47403
www.iuniverse.com
1-800-Authors (1-800-288-4677)

ISBN: 978-1-4917-1264-1 (sc)
ISBN: 978-1-4917-1265-8 (e)

Library of Congress Control Number: 2013919163

Printed in the United States of America.

iUniverse rev. date: 11/15/2013

DEDICATION

To Sensei Robert Koga,
A teacher, a mentor, and most importantly my friend.
You had such a positive impact on countless lives during your lifetime.
Now, through your dedicated students, your spirit will continue to
impact countless more lives by passing on the skills and knowledge
these senior students have learned from you;
Thereby helping keep your dream alive.
"No Give Up"

TRUCK DRIVERS POEM

The Big Rig,
by Dave Madill

There's a tale out on the highway, a legend I've been told,
About a rig that's made of silver, with wheels of solid gold.
There's crosses on the mud flaps, and if you look inside,
Jesus does the driving with St. Peter by his side.
I seen them once in Texas, and another time in Maine,
Once on the roads of ice and snow, and another in the rain.
I know they took a side trip, just to help me find my road,
And proudly I'll go with them when I've pulled my final load.
As I travel down life's highway, I'll do the best I can.
I know that I'm not perfect, I've cheated and I've lied.
But God is forgiving and He knows that I've tried.
I've cheated on my logs, but God knows that's no sin.
With Jesus as my Savior, I know they'll let me in.
So I'll travel down life's highway and when I pull that final mile,
When Jesus stops to pick me up, I'll great him with a smile.
I'll ask if I can drive the rig, with the wheels of solid gold.
He'll toss me the keys and say, "My friend You've Earned This Load".
Then heavens gates will open wide, when they hear that air horn blast,
And the final entry read, the truckers home at last.

TRUCK DRIVER QUOTES

"I don't think I'm bad for people. If I did think I was bad for people, I would go back to driving a truck, and I really mean this."—Elvis Presley

"There is more credit and satisfaction in being a first-rate truck driver than a tenth-rate executive."—B.C. Forbes, Editor and Founder of Forbes Magazine (1917) 1880-1954.

"The truck driver is the lion of the highways, a conquistador sailing upriver in a warship."—Bauvard, the Prince of Plungers

"My father was a truck driver. That's where it all started, and academically I was a disaster at school. My cousin got his name on the honor board; I carved mine on the desk."—Lindsay Fox

"David Bowie, for me, was the butchest guy in town. Jagger was like a truck driver."—Hedi Slimane

"I'm proud of being an Italian-American, but people don't realize that the mafia is just this aberration. The real community is built on the working man, the guy who's the cop, the fireman, the truck driver, the bus driver."—Chazz Palminteri

"I'm an actor . . . . I do a job and I go home. Why are you interested in me? You don't ask a truck driver about his job."—James Gandolfine (Sopranos)

CONTENTS

PREFACE

The purpose *Changing Gears* is to offer those of you who are considering taking up a career in long haul truck driving, some insights and tips to make the transition easier.

I entered the truck driving profession with no experience and no real expectations. I was willing to just go wherever it took me. I am glad I did. I experienced things that I will never forget and carried away some great memories from driving all over the Central and Western United States.

The truck driving profession introduced me to a world I simply did not know existed. Prior to driving an 18-wheeler, I, like most drivers on the highway, would watch the 18-wheelers rolling down the highway, but never give them much thought. My primary thought when seeing one of those big trucks was to either get out of his way, or to pass him. I simply did not want to get stuck behind a slow truck or get hit by something falling off the truck, like a piece of tire that I often would see on the sides of the road that peel off the wheels of these big trucks on occasion.

Beyond that I didn't give the industry or those drivers a second thought. I really didn't know how they got those jobs as a truck driver or what kind of training they went through.

I first went to the Department of Motor Vehicles and obtained the Commercial Drivers Handbook, studied it for a few days, and then aced the written exam to get my Commercial Learners Permit.

I then went through the training at the Commercial Drivers License School, which took two months. I aced the written exams and then practiced for the on-the-road driver test.

It was normal for a student to fail the on-the-road driving test 3 or 4 times before finally passing. It is simply too difficult for the first time driver to pass the actual driving test on the first attempt. There are just too many items for a rookie student to remember. But I am sure there a few out there did pass on their first attempt.

It took me three tries to pass the actual driver test. On my first attempt, I failed to mention some critical areas in the pre-trip inspection. On my second attempt I made a left turn that the instructor felt was too close to an approaching vehicle, forcing said vehicle to brake before the trailer cleared the intersection. I finally passed on my third attempt.

Just making it through the school and testing process was an accomplishment in and of itself.

I then went through two weeks of academic training with Schneider National, having to pass several tests along the way. Then, after passing yet another on-the-road evaluation, I went on to train for two weeks under a 'Training Engineer' in Salt Lake City.

After passing the 'Training Engineer's' evaluation with flying colors, I was finally on my own.

I then drove an 18-wheeler with no violations of any kind and no accidents. Most rookie drivers have some kind of accident or violation in their first few weeks of driving.

After entering this profession, I was surprised with some of the companies, like Schneider National, Stevens Transport, J.B. Hunt, Melton Truck Lines and many others, who seemed committed to raising the bar and developing truly professional drivers. Drivers who not only look professional, but are also true professionals on the road.

There are still a lot of very bad truck drivers out there who drive too fast, follow cars too close and simply drive in a manner that endangers the motoring public. We have all seen them. Well, with the help of some of these good companies and the Department of Transportation's new rules and enforcement tools, the highways should be a lot safer.

In addition, those new drivers coming into the industry will benefit from this increased effort to clean up the transportation industry. Drivers will tend to be better compensated as a result of this attempt to raise the bar in the trucking industry. Those good carriers, in cooperation with the various regulatory agencies, are helping to paint a brighter picture for the trucking industry.

I decided to write this book after failing to find any positive books designed to help the average person, like me, who was considering a career in the trucking industry. There were no books to help me get a better idea of what was involved in driving an 18 wheeler with tips to help shorten the learning curve.

This book is about my experiences, mistakes and subsequent recommendations that others, who may also be considering driving an 18 wheeler, could benefit from.

After reading this book you will have a good idea what is involved in getting a truck driving job, a list of resources to continue your research as well as have a head start from reading about the mistakes and the hard lessons that I experienced.

Good luck, and remember to commit to your new truck driving job for at least one year. It takes at least that long to get a good feel for the job, to pick up all subtleties of the job and to set yourself up for better paying positions in the future.

ACKNOWLEDGEMENTS

After retiring, my wife, Meriam and I decided to move away from San Jose, California, back to Colorado for several reasons. First my youngest daughter, Alyssa, was about to enter middle school. So if we were going to move now was the time to do it.

Moving back to Colorado (I was born there) turned out to be one of the best decisions for me and my family. We made some great friends and had some of the best experiences of our lives.

Secondly, all of my close relatives lived in the Denver and Colorado Springs area. I wanted Alyssa to grow up knowing my oldest daughter, Kristin, (from a different marriage) and her husband Jake (who gave me the title for this book; thanks Jake) and their two sons, Murphy and Ole; my older sister, Kitty, and her husband, 'Uncle Chuckee', my nephew John-Francis, my niece Lisa and her children, Garret and Brady, and all the cousins. I feel they are all some of the nicest people on this earth. So of course, I wanted my daughter get to know them.

Finally, Colorado is one of the most beautiful states I has ever been to. The skiing there is second to none. We grew to love Breckenridge, Colorado. The skiing is fantastic and the small town with all its shops and restaurants are wonderful.

Seven years after moving to Monument, my youngest daughter graduated from high school, and is now attending college and is basically on her own.

At this time I found myself going through withdrawals. I was no longer attending those wonderful club and high school soccer games that my daughter excelled at. I loved watching her play and took thousands of pictures of her soccer games during that 7 year period of middle and high school.

We were no longer attending those great high school ice hockey games (Lewis Palmer/ Palmer Ridge High Schools) with those thrilling games that led to back to back state championships.

No more attending the high school footballs games with my daughter. No more soccer team parties at our home and no more poker parties with the parents. The house was empty and quiet.

This is when I decided to go on a little adventure, and drive an 18 wheeler around the country.

I decided to write this book after failing to find any books designed to help the person who, like me, was considering a career in the trucking industry. There was nothing to help me get a better idea of what was involved in driving an 18 wheeler with tips to help shorten the learning curve.

This book is about my experiences, mistakes and subsequent recommendations that others, who may also be considering driving an 18 wheeler, could benefit from.

CHAPTER 1

DRIVING SCHOOL AND
RELATED TRAINING

I attended school at CDL College in Aurora, Colorado. I choose this particular commercial driving school because they were the only school in the Denver area that had a program that fit my schedule. I was still teaching gymnastics, which limited my availability to attend school. Most commercial driving schools have very rigid programs that force you to take time off from work to attend their program.

CDL College has a very flexible program. I was able to complete the academic part of the course 'on line', which was a huge plus. Being able to go over the on-line material as many times as I wanted to, aided in cementing the academic principles in my mind. As opposed to a classroom setting where you get the information just one time, often rushing through the material and then quickly moving on to the next topic. The on-line approach is much better than a classroom setting on so many levels.

After completing and passing the academic portion, I then had to drive 70 miles round trip to Aurora to do the actually 'behind the wheel' training. This portion of the training involved 3 weeks of driving practice, which could be broken up to fit the students schedule. I attended the driving portion 3 or 4 days a week, depending on my schedule.

This program operated 7 days a week which was another huge plus for the person who is very busy and needs the flexibility of being able to attend on weekends.

Regardless of which truck driving school you attend, be aware that some people qualify for federal or state grants. So check with state officials and the school you choose to obtain more information.

Carriers Who Operate Their Own Driver School

Some trucking companies have their own schools and will train you for free if you sign a contract and work for them for at least one to two years.

I have heard that Stevens Transport School in Dallas, Texas, is a good school. They also have a school in Denver. It is in Stevens's best interest to train you right, since you will be working for them and driving their trucks. I almost went with Stevens Transport, but they just ended up on the wrong side of the coin flip.

If you decide to attend a company's free training, be sure to read these contracts carefully. If you leave their company before the stipulated time is up, you will be responsible for a portion of the cost of the training they put you through. That is only fair.

If you attend one of these company run driving schools, and fail to pass, you may still be responsible for reimbursing the company. So read that contract carefully and ask lots of questions.

No matter what school you go to, take it seriously. Study like your life depends on it. Use your time wisely and try to enjoy your learning experience. If you are returning home after class each day, I recommend you find someplace else to study. The home environment is often filled with distractions; the dogs want attention, your children are constantly interrupting you, your wife is interrupting you, the noise level is high. All this will prevent you from studying and learning the material. Find a library, or coffee shop where you can sit in the corner and focus on your material with no distractions.

If you pay for your own commercial driving school, make sure they have a good job placement program.

In my brief experience, the top two 'break-in' trucking companies for the new commercial driver right out of driving school are Schneider National (www.schneider.com, 1-800-447-7433), and Stevens Transport (www.stevenstransport.com, 1-800-333-8595). Both are very selective on who they will hire.

Compare Benefits of Each Carrier

After reviewing information on several companies including the above two, and pouring over information I found on-line, I decided to go to work for Schneider National. I was impressed with their emphasis on driver safety and they paid the most while you were attending training.

Since I was a new driver, safety was my first concern. I had too many things to learn and think about to be distracted by a company that had a poor reputation. In retrospect, I would have been just as happy with Stevens Transport and actually would have made more money in the long run with Stevens. But I am happy I choose Schneider.

Stevens Transport does primarily refrigerated hauls, and their runs are longer, therefore you make more money. I later learned they are also very serious about driver safety. I also recently found out from one of the company representatives that Stevens Transport does not even carry snow chains in their trucks. Their policy is that they will not send their drivers on routes that require chains; and if chains are required they will either re-route you or have you hunker down until conditions improve. I like that! But, I am still happy I picked Schneider. They are a good company and I had a good experience with them.

While I was on the road I was really impressed with J.B. Hunt trucking company (www.jbhunt.com). I have never had a bad experience with a J.B. Hunt driver, and they were some of the safest drivers on the road. Upon contacting J.B. Hunt, I discovered they will not even consider hiring you until you have at least one year of experience. So, you really need to keep your nose clean and drive safely to even have a chance at one of those companies that are looking for good drivers and are willing to pay you a decent wage.

If you don't mind learning how to drive a flat bed, then Melton Truck Lines (www.meltontruck.com) appears to be a good company. After you graduate from driver school, they will pay you during orientation. Melton was recently named in the "Top 20 Best Fleets to Drive For", according to the Carriers Edge and Truckload Carriers Association and is in the top 1% for pay. They pay recent graduates higher than any other company I could find. They are definitely worth checking out.

I do not want to discourage you from investigating other companies as well. I can only tell you that after meeting drivers from some of these other *break-in* companies that I will not mention in this book, I could not get away from them fast enough. Every single one of them did nothing but complain. Their primary complaints were being treated poorly by their dispatchers, bad equipment, not enough miles and difficulty getting home time when they wanted it. I can't help feel that many of their problems were brought on by their own poor attitude, but some of their criticism probably has some merit.

I remember while I was attending driving school, there was a group of students with us that had already been hired by an oil drilling company. The company was paying for their driving school, after which they were headed to North Dakota, earning up to $80K driving tankers in the oil fields up there. That was very tempting for me, but that is a young man's game up there. Life is rough up there and hours are just as rough. I spent three winters up there in North Dakota while in the Air Force, so I know how cold it gets up there and how that wind will cut right through you. But it is an option for you if that hard life doesn't scare you away.

Do your homework, and go with which ever company you feel comfortable with. You should start your search as soon as you can. Again, there are some companies that conduct their own commercial driving schools (Stevens Transport), and most companies will reimburse you up to $4,000, over a one to two year period, for the costs of putting yourself through a commercial license school.

Be aware that there are some very poor driving schools out there. So if you have decided on a company or are talking with a specific trucking company, go ahead and ask them what driving schools they would recommend in your area, if they don't offer their own school.

If you find a company near your present home that you really like, but they don't hire new drivers, this is what I recommend you do.

Sit down with someone who is in a position to make the hiring decisions or recommendations, like a manager. Let them know you would like to work for their company and are willing to do any work they have and gradually work your way up to a driver position.

If they have nothing for you at the time, go ahead and start working for some 'break-in' company. But whenever you are home, drop by and talk with the manager to let him know you are still interested in working for his company. Also let him know who you are currently driving for.

Be positive in your conversations about your learning experiences. No one will hire a complainer! Ask if you can hang around to learn how their company works, how to hook up 'pups' (small trailers), anything to learn more about the company.

Be enthusiastic! Energetic employees are a manager's dream come true. Believe me, if you are honest and sincere, the manager will think of you when an opening comes up.

CDL Endorsements

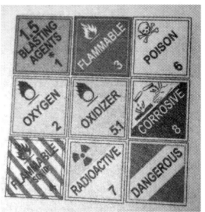

When you finally do get your commercial driver's license, go ahead and study the free DMV booklet and get all the endorsements, i.e., doubles & triples, hazardous material and tankers. Even though you will not be using these endorsements immediately, it looks good on your resume and most *break-in* companies will reimburse you for the costs of getting some of these endorsements.

The hazardous material endorsement is probably the most important because you could possibly be using that endorsement after your first couple months of driving. With that endorsement, it opens you up to being available to haul Hazardous Material loads, which is a good thing. The more diverse your qualifications the more valuable you are to the company and the more loads you qualify for.

One of the surprising things I learned while researching statistics on various violations that truckers are cited for, was the number of citations issued for not having the proper CDL endorsements for the type of vehicle being driven or load being pulled. In 2012 there were 2,021 violations for failure to have the proper endorsements. Come on guys! Everyone knows you need an endorsement on your CDL in order to carry Hazardous Materials, or double/triples or tankers. It is hard to believe a company would allow a driver to operate a vehicle or pull a load that he does not have the proper endorsements for. To me, that is a sign of such laziness and incompetence, they don't belong in the commercial carrier business.

Over The Road Evaluation

I attended Schneider's 3 week new driver orientation and evaluation course in Fontana, California. The first week was mostly academic, going over the way Schneider does business and what is expected from their drivers. Every afternoon, we would also have at least 2-3 hours of behind the wheel review. This included slow maneuvering, backing into tight spaces and over the road practice.

I then went to Salt Lake City to complete my over the road evaluation. I got lucky and was assigned to a great trainer (Training Engineer), Steve Cavanaugh. I had a hell of a time getting the shifting down smooth, but finally got it down with some help from Steve. I will go into shifting a little later in this book.

After passing through the learning curve and becoming comfortable with the equipment and the routines, I liken driving a truck to spending a nice relaxing day tinkering around in the garage all day. It is very relaxing, and time just fly's by as your cruising down the highway.

Riders and Pets

After driving for six months, maybe more, most companies will allow you to bring a spouse or older child with you in the truck. That would be really cool for a teenager on spring break or summer vacation. Check with the companies you are researching to see what their policies are. Some companies even allow you to bring a pet.

Becoming an Independent Operator (IO)

Schneider National has a program that you can qualify for after only 1 year that allows you to purchase a good used truck that is a couple years old, with nothing down and some great terms. Then you can use your computer to pick your own loads, go where you want to go, when you want to go and make 3 to 4 times the money. The vast majority of people I met who were on that program, were very happy with it. The bottom line is you have to be prepared to put in your time before you are eligible for those other driving jobs that not only pay better but give you better home time with dedicated routes that can have you home every night, every other night or at least every weekend.

Since I worked for Schneider National, I looked on their web site, www.schneiderjobs.com, and clicked on the tab at the top labeled 'Owner-Operators', and then clicked on Lease Programs. Schneider offers two types of owner-operator programs;

1. The mileage lease program provides owner operators with the freedom to focus on their driving while Schneider handles the load assignments. This program pays .92 cents a mile and .15 cents per mile performance bonus. But this bonus, as I found out, is not as easy to qualify for as they claim.

2. The percentage lease option provides owner operators the ability to select their own load and decide when and where they want to go. This option gives 65% of the line-haul revenue and 100% of the fuel surcharge to the owner operator. In other words, instead of being tied down to a mileage cap, and depending on a dispatcher to assign you your next load, you pick your own loads and share in the profit the company gets for transporting that load. Owner-operators can make an average of $800.00 per day with some making $1,000.00 per day.

Now you have to understand that as an owner-operator you are responsible for buying your own truck, as well as all the various regulatory and operating costs. You have to be organized and have a strong work ethic.

Personally this percentage option is the one I would go for. After being out there and meeting other drivers and observing their habits and general lack of a good work ethic (yes, there a lot of very lazy drivers out there), I know that I would excel under this program. With my work ethic and understanding of how important it is to stay on top of regulatory matters, I would be a shining star for whatever company I worked for. In addition I really see the benefit of being in charge of your own schedule, picking your own loads to wherever you want to go or picking loads that have the largest financial reward and go wherever those loads take you. Of course it is not always as easy as that, there will be problems picking up loads in certain areas of the country which means you may have to 'dead head' it several miles to get your next load. The term 'dead head' means when the truck is rolling without a load, either with an empty trailer or no trailer, which is called 'Bob Tailing'. You may have to 'Bob Tail' to another location after dropping a trailer at a distributor or warehouse that does not have either an empty or full trailer available for you. This rarely happened to me, but when it did, it was a real benefit working for a large company like Schneider because they have trailers all over the country. You don't have to travel but a few miles to find another trailer.

Then there are the independent truck drivers who are not affiliated with any company. They usually only do live loads and live unload since they own the trailer. Independent drivers have their own company and keep 100% of the line-haul revenue.

The other truck companies I mention in this book also have similar programs. Schneider is not the only game in town. I am just more familiar with them and had a good experience with them. They all offer good training and support to help you succeed at whatever level you want to participate at.

$1 Million Government Grant

On July 1, 2013, the U.S. Department of Transportation announced a $1 Million grant to help train Veterans for transportation jobs. The money will go to six colleges across the country as part of the Commercial Motor Vehicle Operator Safety Training Grant Program. The colleges involved with this grant are as follows:

- Century College in Minneapolis/ St. Paul, Minnesota.
- Grays Harbor College in Aberdeen, Washington.
- Long Beach Community College in Long Beach, California.
- Orangeburg-Calhoun Technical College in Orangeburg, South Carolina.
- Lone Star College in Woodlands, Texas.
- Joliet College in Joliet, Illinois.

Final Advice

Regardless which trucking company you settle on, try to stick it out with the same company for the entire year. If you jump around from one company to another, it simply indicates you do not have the 'stick with it' mentality that a lot of companies like to see.

That is why it is important to take your time and do your homework. Remember you can start to call the *'break in'* companies long before you go to school to get your commercial driver's license. If you are going to pay for your own schooling, it gives you a little more freedom in regards to which company to work for.

I hope that the Truck Driving industry in the United States moves toward a salary based system instead of mileage, similar to how drivers in Europe are paid. That would be a much fairer system than the current one, which is very difficult for the new driver to make a livable wage at. I remember those times when my truck broke down, and I was stuck where ever I was, making no money! I only got about $25 a day as break down compensation. In the long run you would make just as much flipping burgers at a fast food restaurant. But, then again, flipping hamburgers does not give you the long term possibilities that commercial driving offers.

CHAPTER 2

COMPANY ORIENTATION

Qualcomm®

When you are finally hired by a trucking company, most company orientation sessions focus on teaching you the specific way they conduct business. That includes orientation in the *Qualcomm®*, which is a company in San Diego, CA. that developed and owns the communication device, usually situated on the dash board of the truck, and used by several trucking companies. Theses devises are used to communicate with the truck, allows the driver to communicate with his dispatcher and gives turn by turn directions to each destination, as well other functions. This device has changed trucking for the better and has made it a lot easier for the new driver to be successful as well as reducing the stress of finding your destination.

Workflow System

During your company training, you will be introduced to some kind *of' Workflow system'*. It is a little confusing at first, but don't worry, you will begin to understand the fine points in no time at all. I will not try to address these systems, as they are constantly changing and improving each day. Even the instructors were not up on the latest updates when I was going through my orientation. Just practice every chance you get and prepare before you go to this class by reading your material on this subject.

Come to Training Prepared to Study

While you are attending the company training, do yourself a favor and focus on why you are there. The company orientation is usually two weeks long, with an additional one or two weeks for 'on the road' time with a Training Engineer (TA). This orientation is NOT just a formality. You can still be 'cut' and advised to go home and try again later. You should come to the training prepared to do nothing but read and study all the information they give you. You are there on their dime, so show them some respect by doing your part to prepare yourself. That means when they release you to go back to your hotel, forget about the 'Social Scene". Get your ass into the books and materials they provide and start learning or reviewing that material.

The training will be a lot less stressful if you focus on studying the materials as they give them to you, not at the last minute. Don't fall into the trap of getting home or back to the hotel and just relaxing by the pool or begin to watch TV. There is plenty of time for that later.

If you want to get started in this career with as few glitches as possible, work, study and practice every chance you can. The instructors have a lot of material to cover with very little time to review. In addition, don't take it personal if the instructors can't remember your name. They literally go through hundreds of students every month or two and simply can't remember everybody.

The vast majority of students they go through will eventually wash out with-in 6 months. They either quit or are fired after getting into a preventable accident. If you want to have a better chance of being part of that small percentage that makes it to the one year mark, pay attention during your training and apply everything you learn.

CHAPTER 3

TRAINING ENGINEER/ ON THE ROAD TRAINER

The Training Engineer is an experienced company driver, specially trained and tasked with giving you the opportunity to take on all the responsibilities of a driver; from viewing and deciphering the incoming pre-assignment messages, trip planning, confirming or accepting the assignment, doing the pre-trip and post-trip inspections, dropping and hooking trailers, long distance driving, navigating truck stops, how to fuel the truck, how to scale your load and so much more. Some trainers are sincere and want to help you learn as many skills as you can; some trainers are simply in it for the extra money and have no real interest in training you. No matter which one you end up with, it is YOUR responsibility to ask questions. Be a pain in the ass if necessary, to let the trainer know that you expect to take on all the responsibilities with the truck and trailer, under his supervision. That is the best way to learn. You will learn very little if all you do is watch the instructor for a week. It may be tempting to just sit back and watch the instructor the whole week, because of your lack of confidence in yourself and the normal desire to not look foolish.

Once you get out on the road on your own, you will panic because you never really did all the activities necessary to successfully drop & hook trailers, proper Qualcomm procedures, accepting pre-assignments, how to trip plan before accepting the assignment, making sure you have all the hours necessary to complete the delivery, and on and on.

When I began my training with my Schneider Training Engineer, Steve Cavanaugh, he drove the truck to the first assignment. I went inside the shipper's office with him to pick up the paperwork, at which point he threw the truck keys to me and said," OK, it's all yours from now on". I never did thank him for forcing me to go through that really uncomfortable learning curve. So, if you're still out there Steve, thanks for being a great trainer. Thanks to Steve I was as prepared as I could be for my first solo load.

When I picked up my first truck after my 'On the Road' training, I was fairly confident. While I was in my truck preparing for my first load, there happened to be one of my classmates in the same company lot, <u>trying</u> to prepare to pick up his first assignment as well. He did not really study, was unfortunately stuck with a bad trainer and was subsequently completely frozen in the truck seat. He was staring at the Qualcomm screen, completely lost. He was so stressed out. He could not remember how to do anything because he had never really done it with his instructor. So, please take every opportunity to do everything with your 'over the road' instructor. It will pay huge dividends as you start accepting and pulling your own load.

Pup Trailers

As a side note, while I was going through my training in Salt Lake City, I had a lot of down time while I sat in the truck at the Schneider yard. I watched drivers come and go, trying to glean what I could just by watching. I noticed these smaller trailers just sitting in the middle of the yard. I was later advised that these smaller trailers were called 'pups'. These 'pups' were about 28 feet long, as compared to the 52 foot regular trailers. I remembered reading about 'pups' when I studied for my learners permit. I remember reading about how these 'pups' connect to each other with a dolly, and the dangers and procedures of pulling double and triples when I was studying for my doubles & triples CDL endorsements.

As I was just sitting in my truck, I noticed this Schneider driver pull into the yard and start to work with these pup trailers. I got out and struck up a conversation with him (always trying to learn something new) and he was more than willing to explain how the pups worked, the way they are hitched to each other with a dolly and the dangers of doing it incorrectly.

The reason I bring this up is that it turns out most better paying trucking jobs I mention later in this book use these 28 foot trailers 'pups' a lot. So I highly recommend getting whatever experience you can with these pup trailers while you can. If the break-in company you end up going to work for uses pup's, volunteer to help hook and unhook them, after proper instruction of course. Take every opportunity to talk to the drivers who are pulling these pups. They more than likely will be glad to tell you everything they know about them and how they operate. Down the road when you are ready to make a change to a better paying position, you will be able to tell them that you are familiar with pups and how they go together.

Less than Truckload (LTL) Companies

I would recommend researching your home town area for any 'LTL— Less Than Truck Load' trucking companies. If you find any, I would use your days off to go down, introduce yourself and let them know that you just started driving, or if you have not started yet, that you are interested in a driving career and that you would like to see how they operate, especially the 28 foot pup trailers. My bet is that they will be more than happy to let you tag along with one of the drivers who will give you an education you will never forget. You never know, they may be impressed enough with you and tell you to come back when you have 6 months experience and they may have a job for you. Opportunities are not going to look for you, YOU have to go out and make it happen. The more you do it, the more comfortable it will feel.

CHAPTER 4

DRIVING SKILLS AND SHIFTING

When I actually started to drive on the freeways, especially in crowed city driving, I had problems staying in my lane. My instructor kept telling me, "Hold your lane", as I began to drift into an adjacent lane. I discovered that I was focusing my vision too close to the front of the truck, about 100 feet, making my lane drifting corrections to quick and severe. What I eventually learned was that, while driving freeway speeds, if you focus your vision at least 500 feet in front of the truck, it is very natural and easy to keep your corrections very subtle, and to stay in the middle of your lane.

This holds true for turns as well. Focus well enough ahead of the truck to know just how the turn is changing. By the time you get to that change in the turn you have already begun your adjustment. For left sweeping freeway turns, focus on the line on the driver's side. Don't drive too close to it or your trailer make drift into the lane on your left. For right sweeping freeway turns, focus on the right line, the lane adjacent to the passenger side of the truck. But as I mentioned above, don't drive too close to this line, as you trailer may cross over it and hit something.

The driving school will teach you all this, but I found that once I was on the road by myself, I had so many things I was thinking about and trying to pay attention to, I often forgot about these basic techniques.

Mirrors

One of those basic things you should understand right off the bat is to make sure your mirrors are properly adjusted. There were a few times I would start to change lanes and fail to see the car next to my cab. This occurred because I did not have my mirrors adjusted correctly. When I was driving, my truck used what they call a West Coast mirror and Spot mirror, as well as the fender mirrors. Make sure you use ALL three mirrors. When I first started driving I failed to use the fender mirrors as often as I should have.

Make sure the bracket that the mirrors are attached to be positioned at a 90 degree angle to the truck, which places the mirrors at their farthest point from the truck. Adjust your main mirror so that as you sit in your seat you should NOT be able to see the side of the trailer. In order to see the trailer you simply lean back slightly. If you have to lean way back before you see the side of the trailer, then you need to adjust the mirror so that just a slight lean back will give you a view of the side of your trailer. The spot mirror located directly under the main mirror, should be adjusted out as far as you can get it. You should still be able to see the side of the cab and trailer, but you will have a better view of what is in the lane next to your cab and trailer.

Then we have the Fender mirrors. These mirrors are critical to view what may be right next to your cab. These need to be adjusted so that you can see only a little of the side of your truck. Only ¼ or less of you mirror should be taken up with the side of your truck and steps, the rest of what you see in the mirror should reveal the space next to your cab and trailer.

Slow Down On Curves

Equally important is the speed at which you are traveling when entering curves. The speed limits posted on curves and freeway ramps are designed for automobiles, not big trucks. Sometimes you will see speed limit signs posted for trucks, but not often. In the short time I was driving a truck, I saw at least 3 accidents on freeway off ramps, where it was obvious the truck was going too fast for the ramp and tipped over.

In my own case, there were at least two occasions where I approached an off ramp to fast. In both circumstances I had some idiot truck driver who was behind me and approaching the same ramp, but way too fast. This driver was right on my DOT bumper. I did not slow down as much as I should have and took the off ramp 5-10 M.P.H. over the posted speed limit trying to avoid being rear ended by the other trucker.

Yes, there are lots of very bad truck drivers out there. What you need to realize is that they do not pay your salary. They do not care about you. DO NOT let them bully you into driving in an unsafe manner. Once you have finished your training and have a few months of experience, you will have a better idea of how to drive safely. The best thing to do is ignore those unsafe drivers and drive the way you were trained. Those unsafe drivers will eventually get what they deserve and will lose their commercial licenses.

The tractor and trailers have a high center of gravity, so it doesn't take much to tip them over. In three cases I saw trucks taking freeway ramps too fast when it was raining. The first truck turned his front wheels, but the pavement was too slick and the entire truck jackknifed and kept going straight, right off the road and 200 feet into the grassy field. He was very lucky there was not a steep embankment or a solid wall in his path.

In another event, the trucker lost traction while going too fast on an off ramp and slammed into the guardrail. The guardrail was so crumpled it looked like the Green Hulk used it to demonstrate how badly he could destroy and crush a guardrail.

The third accident I saw happened about a half mile ahead of me on a long 3 mile downhill slope. This driver made an abrupt lane change from the middle lane to the off ramp and lost traction. It had just started raining real hard and the roads were especially slick. I don't know if he survived, but his truck definitely did not survive. He slide head on into the beginning of a guard rail, went over the rail and took out over 100 feet of railing. He luckily stopped just on the edge of an embankment down into a river. His truck and trailer were ripped open.

17

I was reading an article in one of the industry publications, where they were interviewing a veteran driver who tipped his truck and trailer on a freeway on ramp. He said he really didn't think he was going that fast. The accident upset him so much, and he was so embarrassed, he decided to retired the next week. He stated it was so easy to get complacent, and make wrong assumptions.

I overheard an instructor say that some of the worst accidents are actually caused by veteran drivers who have just become complacent. Some of these drivers were multi-million mile award winning drivers.

I hope you glean the message from these few examples. It should be very clear. As you become more proficient and comfortable driving a truck, don't get complacent.

My message here is to slow down at least 5 to 10 mph below the posted speed limit on curves and at least 10 to 15 mph below the posted limit if the pavement is wet or icy. Most freeway ramps are designed so that the curve gets sharper the further you get into the curve. So it may not look that sharp initially, but before you know it you find yourself going way too fast for the middle part of the curve.

Loading Docks

One additional item that I personally did not have an issue or problem with, but is important to mention, involves rules around the docks of various shippers. All of the docks I have ever been to, have some kind of restrictions on the driver to prevent him from mistakenly pulling out of the dock before the trailer is completely loaded. It seems like a no brainer to me, but I just don't understand how someone could 'mistakenly' think that the trailer was loaded and then just pull out without checking with someone to insure all the loaders were done. But some docks have gone to what I think are extreme measures to keep drivers from leaving too early. But, on second thought, any procedures or rules that make the work place safer for those loaders are fully justified.

Most docks require you to chock your wheels. They will have rubber or steel wedges for you to place in front of you trailer tires. This prevents you from just pulling out without removing the chocks, and you don't remove the chocks until the dock personnel advise you that it is ok to pull them out and pull away from the dock.

Some docks have a hook that grabs the rear of the trailer once you are backed in completely. Obviously this will prevent you from pulling out too early as your trailer is locked into the dock.

A few docks require you to bring your truck keys into the warehouse and either hang them on a board or give them to a specified person. Once your trailer is loaded, they will return your keys.

Some docks do not want you to leave your truck while they load it, while others require you to sit in a designated area in the warehouse until they are finished with loading your trailer.

Many docks have a light system that works like a traffic signal. As you back into your assigned dock, you will see a green light in your driver side mirror. This light is adjacent to the door you are backing into. Once you are positioned correctly, and your wheels are chocked, they will begin to load your trailer. At this point, just before they begin to load your trailer, that light will turn red. As long as that light is red, don't move the trailer, because they have personnel driving forklifts or pulling pallet Jacks in or out of the trailer putting their product in or pulling product out of your trailer. Once the light is green again, it is the warehouses signal to you that they are finished and you can now pull the trailer out.

In any case, regardless of what system they have, NEVER pull a trailer away from a dock until you have personally confirmed that the trailer is ready to be moved and no one is still inside.

Trailer Doors

There was one step in this process of pulling into the loading docks that I continued to have problems with. It was more of a mental error, but still slowed me down unnecessarily. So I will discuss it here in hopes you don't make the same mental error.

You must have your trailer doors open <u>before</u> you can completely back into the dock. If you don't, the trailer doors will not open because they are jammed up against the dock. In addition, if you have other trailers also parked in the dock on one or both side of you trailer, you may not have enough room to swing the doors open.

Depending on the procedure at the warehouse you are pulling into, you will need to have the trailer doors open <u>before</u> you back into the dock. If your trailer is loaded and has a seal on it DO NOT remove the seal until you have been instructed to do so. Often the guard will verify the seal in intact and then remove it for you or instruct you to go ahead and remove it. After the trailer doors are open, you can back the trailer into the dock.

Shipping Scenario-Empty Trailer

Let me walk through a common scenario you will go through at a typical warehouse. Let's say you have an empty trailer and you are pulling into the shipper's facility. As you approach the guard shack, there are often signs posted with various tasks you need to do before getting to the gate, like 'sliding your tandems all the way to the rear'. As the guard shack is dealing with the truck in front of you, put your parking brakes on, get out of the truck, and walk to the rear of your trailer. Reach in and pull out the locking bar that allows the large pins that keep your tandems (trailer wheels) locked into the frame, to retract. Make sure the bar in locked in the open position and all four pins are retracted. Get back into your truck, release only the truck brakes, leaving the trailer brakes engaged. You don't want the trailer being able to move. Keeping the trailer brakes engaged allows you to slide the trailer over the rear tandems forward or backward, depending on what you are trying to do. In this case you have an empty trailer, so you will need to <u>slowly</u> pull the truck forward until you here and feel the rear tandems lock all the way to the rear. Set your brakes, walk to the back and verify the tandems are locked to the rear.

Warehouses want your trailer wheels/tandems to be all the way to the rear because in that position, when the forklifts are driving in and out of the trailer, having the wheels to the rear will mitigate the bounce and movement of the trailer, making it safer to load and unload.

Now you have your trailer tandems slide all the way to the rear and locked into that position. Since you have an empty trailer you will either be getting that trailer loaded at the dock, which is what we call a *live* load or you will be dropping that empty trailer wherever they tell you to drop it.

With a *live load* you will be waiting while they load your trailer. In the other scenario, after you drop your empty trailer, the shipper will have a *pre-loaded trailer* waiting for you. Let's address both scenarios.

First, you pull up to the guard shack with an empty trailer and as part of your assignment that you reviewed when you accepted this load you know that this is a *'drop and hook'*. In other words you will be dropping the empty trailer you are pulling, on the shipper's property and then will pick up a pre-loaded trailer.

The guard will ask you for your commercial driver's license and specific information, i.e., load number, shipping number that was included in you load assignment. You should have written down all this information on a tablet when you received this assignment. These are all steps your 'on the road trainer' should teach you.

After checking his computer, the guard will tell you where to drop the empty and then where to pick the loaded trailer. The guard will often give you a map of the facility and circle the spot they want you to drop the empty as well as give you the trailer number of your loaded trailer and the space number where it is located. The guard will give you specific instructions on where to go and what to do. Drop the trailer in the space number they gave you, then, sometimes you may have to go to the shipping office to get the shipping papers before picking up the loaded trailer. But again, the guard's job is to tell you what the procedures are.

Once you have picked up the loaded trailer, have verified it is the correct trailer number and the seal number corresponds to the seal number recorded on the shipping papers, you are almost ready to hit the road. Make sure to do a complete inspection of the trailer to insure it is safe to move and has no defects that would prevent it from safely being pulled on the highway.

Flat Tire on Trailer

There have been several occasions where I have had to pick up loaded trailers with flat tires, torn or broken air lines (no brakes!) or with severe damage to the trailer itself. Make sure to document any damage. If you run across these types of problems, call you dispatcher immediately and advise him of the problem. In the case of the flat tire, I recommend you purchase a 'glad hand air hose'. This is simply a 50 foot air hose that hooks up to your air supply. You can use that air pressure generated by the truck to put enough air in your tire to get the trailer to the shop to fix the tire. Your company will have contracts with specific tire centers and will want you to take the defective tire there to get repaired or replaced.

The only things left to do now is to put your own pad lock on the trailer, pull up to the guard shack, and show the guard your paperwork. The guard will check the seal as well, and then he will wave you on your way.

Live Load

Now, let's assume that in this next scenario you have an empty trailer and are scheduled for a *live load*. In other words you will pull into one of their docks with your empty trailer, and they will load it for you.

After reviewing your paperwork, the guard will tell which dock to back into. Remember to open your trailer doors prior to backing into the dock and at some point slide your tandems to the rear.

In this particular scenario, I might wait until I was within a few feet of the dock (backing in) before I slide the tandems to the rear. I do this because the trailer is easier to maneuver into a dock when the rear wheels are slide forward under the trailer. The trailer responds quicker to minor adjustments in that position. Once I have the trailer straight and lined up perfectly with the dock, I stop, slide my tandems to the rear, and then finish my backing maneuver into the dock. Of course I have already opened my trailer doors before I start my backing procedure into the dock while I still have room for the trailer doors to swing open.

They will load your trailer and let you know when it is completed, at which point you will you will pull out of the dock a little, check the load to make sure it is secured properly to mitigate any shifting in the load while you are driving. Then close the doors and they will apply a seal to the door or they may give you the seal to place on the door. Make sure the seal number is correctly recorded on your shipping papers.

At this point some companies will have you put a *company padlock*, sometimes referred to as a' *war lock'*, on the trailer door to help secure the contents from theft. You are given this lock to use on every load you get. Just remember, once you get the load to its destination, REMOVE the lock. I have lost several locks on loads where the loaded trailer was dropped in a given spot, to be unloaded later. But I forgot to take my lock off. In every case, as soon as you pull up to the guard shack at your destination, make it part of your routine to remove the lock while you are stopped at the guard shack or after you slide the tandems to the rear.

Whatever you do, start developing a systematic way of performing your required tasks. That way you are less likely to forget or miss a critical task, like forgetting to remove your personal lock from the loaded trailer.

When I was an investigator, I was trained by Bob Koga to search suspects in a systematic manner so I was less likely to miss any critical areas where the subject might be concealing a weapon. If I did not have a system to follow, and just searched in a random manner every time, I would have been more likely to miss a critical area and thereby miss a possible weapon. I search the same pattern every time, with few exceptions, so I did not have to 'think' about which area I had searched and which I didn't. I search the same way every time, so it frees me up to concentrate on important things like my surroundings, other nearby suspects, etc.

The same principal applies to routines you follow to inspect your truck and trailer or preparing to drop and pick up trailers. Perform specific tasks in a systematic manner, and you will mitigate your chances of forgetting a critical task.

Remember, when sliding your tandems to the rear, pull the rod to unlock the pins, keep the trailer brakes on, release the truck brakes and then slowly drive the truck forward until the tandems lock to the rear. Then release the trailer brakes, and finish your backing until you bump the dock or drop the trailer in a designated location.

Shifting

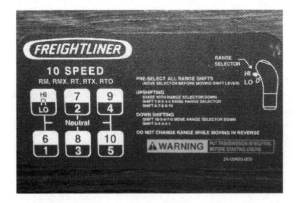

Shifting took me far too long to master. By the time I got it down, I was able to look back and just shake my head in disbelief at just how easy shifting is. When you are driving 40 tons, your mind just thinks that shifting is going to be a real physical challenge, and that is how I approached it. When instructors would make comments on my hard shifting, I just did not understand what they were asking me to do.

Let me tell you now, treat shifting like a lesson in meditation. Keep it soft and relaxed. I know it is hard to believe, but it is true. I drove a 2010 Freightliner Cascadia, with 10 forward gears. Here is what I would tell a new student: "Think of the gearshift shaft, the steel rod that the gear shift handle is attached to, as if it is made of glass. Start off in 2nd or 3rd gear. You rarely need 1st gear except to pull a fully loaded trailer out of a steep loading dock. Shift your gears in the LOWER range of the recommended RPM range given in your guidelines. Don't wait until your engine revolutions are too high. That will just screw you up and cause you to try and force it into gear. You are not on a race track. Take it slow and shift up often. Only depress the clutch enough to get the truck out of the gear it is in and again only 2 or 3 inches to get it into the next upper gear. Often you will not need to depress the clutch at all to get it into the next gear, if done right. This is called *floating gears* and is sometimes discouraged by instructors teaching new students. Trucks shift nothing like my old 1969 Pontiac GTO. I unfortunately tried to shift the truck just like my old GTO, which just led to lots of stress and failure.

One of the shifting techniques I was taught about 3 months after I started was *'skip shifting'*, which is absolutely wonderful. I wished it had been taught to me a long time ago, but as my instructors told me, we can only teach you so much. After you digest and master the basics we can progress from there. You have to learn how to walk before you can run. With skip shifting you skip every other gear until you get up to the point where you engage the selector button for the upper gears. Let me give you an example. If you start off in 2nd gear, you would run your rpm's up to about 1500. Then slow down your double clutch technique, and slowly shift into 4th gear. Your rpm's should drop to 600 by the time you shift into the next gear. So the entire shifting sequence would take about 2 seconds. I know that seems like a long time, but trust me, keep it slow and even. Count out, one thousand one, one thousand two in a slow relaxed speed. From the time you depress the clutch to take the truck out of 2nd gear, start counting. Once you get to the end of "one thousand two", you should just be slipping the gear into 4th. Then continue the same pace, bring rpm's up to about 1600, put your selector switch in the up position, then slowly shift into 6th gear as your rpm's drop to 600. From that point you are in the higher gears and can only shift one gear at a time due to the larger difference between the higher gears. This can also be done from 3rd gear to 5th gear, put selector switch up and shift to 7th gear. Once you get to those higher gears, you need to revert back to single gear shifting. Practice this skip shifting only when you are on a level surface or a slight downgrade. Don't do skip shifting when driving up a slight grade or hill. You will lose too much speed by the time you get into the next gear and then be in a gear that is too high for your speed and you may stall.

There are other shifting techniques like power down shifting where you go from 9th to 7th. I would use this technique when traffic is slowing a little and I want to keep the truck moving, but at a slower speed. There is also the bump and run used to shift from 8th or 9th gear to 4th or 5th gear to slow for a curve, railroad tracks or a traffic light that I anticipate will turn green soon and I don't want to have to come to a complete stop. The key in both of these downshifting techniques is to decrease your speed and rpm's appropriate for the gear you will shift into next.

With all these techniques, practice is the only way to master them. Be patient with yourself and seek help from your operations center training staff if you continue to struggle in this area. Once you get it, you will have that Eureka moment and kick yourself for not picking up on the subtle points of shifting sooner.

Remember, trying to shift in a tense or panic state of mind will only result in frustration and gears not going in smoothly. Shift in a slow, sleepy manner, and you will be much more successful. The transmission of a big commercial truck is just a machine designed to operate a certain way. It does not respond to brute force or verbal threats. You can yell and scream all you want, it does not hear you. Remember what I said at the beginning; shift a big rig like you are taking a lesson in meditation. Relax and let the gears shift with as little effort as you can allow yourself to muster.

Never allow your eyes to leave the road while shifting. Never look down to look at the gear shift knob. You should practice often and always know what gear you are in. Granted, this will take time, but if you don't want the instructors yelling at you, learn to remember what gear you are in at all times so you know what gear you have to go to in order to slow down. You will create a lot of unnecessary stress by attempting to downshift into a gear that is inappropriate for the speed you are traveling at. You will then panic because it won't go into the gear you want, causing you to take your eyes off the road to try and determine what gear it is in and what gear you can downshift into at the speed you are currently going. This is just as bad a looking down to check a text message, but this time you are behind the wheel of 40 tons and can literally crush vehicles and their occupants. So try to get the shifting pattern down in whatever truck you will be driving and always remember what gear you are currently in. You can tell what gear you are in by the sound of the engine, rpm's and your current speed. I know this will take time, but it will become as natural as walking and chewing gum before you know it.

CHAPTER 5

PAPER & ELECTRONIC LOGGING

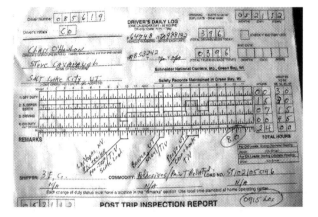

As a professional driver, the Department of Transportation (DOT) requires you to account for every hour of every day you are a driver for any trucking company. This includes your days off.

Why Logging is Required

Before these *HOS (Hours of Service)* rules and paper logs were put in place, commercial truck drivers had few restrictions on how long they could drive. While talking with some old truckers about the new DOT hours of service, they become nostalgic about the good old days when driving use to be 'fun'. These old drivers complain that trucking is no longer fun because it has become over regulated.

The fact is that the lack of regulation decades ago led to drivers putting in a lot of hours behind the wheel. The trucking companies simply wanted to get the product to its destination as quickly as possible. If the driver ended up driving 15 hours straight, no one really thought that was a problem. Those excessive driving hours directly led to accidents due to fatigue from lack of sleep.

Even after some of these rules were put in place, some 'bad' trucking companies continued to encourage their drivers to break these rules. DOT cracked down on these 'bad' companies and tightened up on their rules to the point where we are today.

Now the trucking industry is heavily regulated, many say it is over regulated. I believe, as is sometimes the case, this 'over regulation' is primarily due to the industry's inability and failure to regulate itself. So, DOT stepped in and, for the safety of the motoring public, started clamping down on the bad trucking companies.

Paper logs have been required for a several years now. The newer electronic logs have only been around about 5 years, and have become very popular within the last 2 years, and may become mandatory in the near future. Many of the independent truckers I met on the road still like the paper logs, because they said it is easier to cheat on their hours. Most admitted to keeping two sets of paper logs. It may be for that reason that DOT is considering making electronic logs mandatory. Most of the large established motor carriers have gone to the electronic logging, because it is easier to assist drivers in their efforts to keep from violating their *HOS (Hours of Service)*.

Benefits of Electronic Logging

Electronic logging, from an administrative point of view, is an easier way for a company to keep tabs on their drivers and for drivers to monitor their own hours. All the way around, electronic logging in the trucking industry is a big positive. The only exceptions are those independent drivers who don't want to be told how long they can drive. Electronic logging has helped level the playing field, so to speak, and has made the highways safer by making it more difficult to cheat on your Hours of Service (HOS).

According to the Federal Motor Carrier Safety Administration (FMCSA), they expect a Rule mandating the use of electronic on-board recorder/ electronic log by September of 2013. MAP-21, the highway funding law passed in the summer of 2012, requires FMCSA to implement an electronic log requirement.

This chapter is not meant to teach you how to complete a daily log. The company you end up working for will offer their own training on these skills. What I will do is give you a basic outline of what your *'Drivers Daily Log'*, also referred to as a *'paper log'*, consists of.

Why learn Paper Logs?

While you are in training you will probably have to complete paper logs. This is necessary because you <u>will</u> have to know how to <u>properly</u> complete a paper log. Until you have been issued a *'Driver Number'* by your company, you will not be able to complete your logs electronically. Starting off with paper logs before transitioning to the electronic logs is critical because if, for whatever reason, your electronic logging device goes down, you are still required by law to continue logging your activity and status. You must be familiar with paper logs and how to properly fill them out. You will be required to carry paper logs in your truck. Until the electronic system is back up and running, you are required to account for your time using the paper logs. Failure to log your activity is a violation and can result in a citation.

Log Violations

As you will see near the end of this book I have compiled some statistics in regards to violations. One of the statistics that really surprised me, showed that the number of <u>log related</u> violations (paper & electronic) discovered for 2012 alone (U.S. only/ excluding Canada and Mexico) during roadside inspections, was 436,686. That is all due to pure laziness on the part of the driver and lack of proper training. The citations those drivers received for all those various log related violations were 100% preventable. As you go through your initial training with the company that hires you, pay attention. It really is not that difficult and can result in a citation when you get lazy and fail to properly log your time as required. Repeated logging violations by a driver also impact the carrier. Any violation by a driver can and will reflect on the carrier. Carriers can and will fire a driver who continues to put the company in a bad position with the various regulatory agencies.

Driver Number

When you are hired by a trucking company or *'motor carrier'* which is the legal term, you will be issued a *'Driver Number'*. You will use that *'Driver Number'* on your *driver's daily log,* completing you *electronic Log,* refueling your truck and communicating with your company. The *Driver Number* is a 6 digit number.

The *Drivers Daily Log* has 4 lines you use to report or account for your time. The first is *'off duty'*. This is the time spent when you had no driver responsibilities, like meals, sleeping at a hotel, on vacation, at home on time off, etc. The second line is *'Sleeper Berth'*. If you are off duty but in the *'Sleeper Berth'*, this is where you would record that time. Third line is *'Driving'*. Whenever you are behind the wheel driving, even stuck in traffic, that time would be recorded on this line. The forth line is *'On Duty'*. This would be time when you are performing duties other than driving, i.e., pre/post trip inspections, TIV's, training or classroom activities, etc.

Now these are very general explanations and are subject to slightly different interpretations depending on what your company tells you. This area is constantly changing.

Log 'On Duty' Before or After Pre-Trip Inspection?

What is so nice about *electronic logging* is that most of the entries are automatically done for you. When you log on in the morning, your 14 hour clock starts and does not stop. Once you log on, you have 14 hours to get 11 hours of driving in, which leaves you 3 hours of miscellaneous on duty time to complete your inspections, fueling, etc. Off duty status DOES NOT stop the 14 hour clock. With electronic logging, you are initially logged on as being *On Duty*. At this time you would conduct your *'Pre-Trip Inspection'*. This inspection must take at least 15 minutes, but should take longer. If you log on, then only take 5 minutes to conduct your beginning of the day *'Pre-Trip* Inspection' and then start driving, the *'electronic* log' will not register your inspection. Weeks later you may be questioned as to why you did not perform the required *'pre-trip inspection'*. You of course will swear up and down that you always do your *'Pre-Trip Inspections'*. The problem is that the electronic log will not register it if you don't take at least 15 minutes of your initial *'On Duty'* status to conduct your inspection. So save yourself the headache by always conducting a good solid *'Pre-Trip Inspection'* after logging *'On Duty'*.

Now, in regards to what I just told you above, I have heard of drivers who got up after their required 10 hour break, logged On Duty, jumped out of the truck, and conducted their Pre-Trip Inspection. During that inspection they found a problem that required the company to send out a repair crew. By the time the repair crew got there and fixed the problem, six hours had been burned on their fourteen hour clock. Once you log on, your fourteen hour clock starts and does not stop for any reason. Now this driver only had 5 hours of driving time available which completely screwed up their arrival time and put a real damper on their pay for that day, as they were only able to drive 200 miles that day.

With this in mind, I began to conduct my pre-trip inspection before I logged On Duty. Then, if no problems were discovered that would delay my departure, I would log On Duty after the inspection. I would then spend about 20 minutes working in the truck or checking my e-mail. Then I would finish completing my electronic logging, and hit the road. I know this seem like cheating, but it saves me from wasting an entire day if I find a major problem with the truck or trailer that requires immediate attention. In this case, after the problem is fixed, I still have a good eleven hours of driving ahead of me.

Log Falsifications

As my instructors use to drill into us during the training I received on completing daily logs, 'Log It as You Do It'. In other words, as you perform your daily functions, simply log it as you go along. That is the best way to avoid *'log falsifications'* which is when supporting documents, such as roadside inspection documents, toll receipts, fuel records, other receipts, are compared to your log and there is a discrepancy of either location and/or duty status. Any number of these 'log falsifications' could lead to you getting fired. The last thing a good company needs is a driver who continually lies on his logs. These types of violations can impact the trucking company as well as you. I recently read about two trucking companies that were shut down by DOT due to repeated logging violations of by its' drivers. So carriers have everything to lose by turning a blind eye to drivers who repeatedly violate the Federal Motor Carrier Safety Regulations. You can see these enforcement actions on the DOT and FMCSA web sites. Look for them under the 'Press Release' tab.

Generally logging is done is 15 minute chunks. Make sure you keep up on your logging, especially with paper logs. Before you know it, a few hours have gone by and you may get stuck guessing what you did and when you did it. The same holds true with electronic logging. As long as you perform your duties like your suppose to, and complete your electronic logging as taught, you should have no problems. Always approach your job with honesty and integrity. If you have questions, discuss them with your dispatcher or whoever they assign to discuss issues and problems that come up. When I worked for Schneider National, they assigned me a Driver Business Leader (DBL). As mentioned earlier, I got lucky and was assigned Greg Russell in Salt Lake City. He was very good!

Electronic Log Status Changes/ Minimize Wasting 'On Duty' Hours

Within the first couple miles of driving your truck, you are automatically logged on to the *'Driving'* line. You can also manually log on to the *'Driving'* line as well, which some trainers prefer. If you don't manually log on to the driving line, and have an accident while merging on to the freeway, before the electronic log can log you on the driving log, you technically have a log falsification.

When you stop the truck, and turn off the engine, the electronic log automatically changes your status from 'Driving' to *'On Duty'* unless you manually change it to *'Off Duty'*. So, if you pull into a truck stop to fuel, and plan on eating a meal at that location, make sure after you fuel and park your truck and trailer, to manually change your status to *'Off Duty'* or the electronic log will keep you *'On Duty'*, and burn up valuable time.

My point here is that *'Electronic logging'*, as opposed to paper logs, is much more accurate, efficient and makes it easier to comply with DOT regulations. There a couple tricks to help you stretch your 60 or 70 hour *'On Duty'* clock, which involves making sure you log *'Off Duty'* (as mentioned above) whenever you stop to eat, load and unload, whenever you have no work or truck related responsibilities. Basically it involves just <u>remembering</u> to log 'off duty' when it is appropriate, as opposed to burning up those on duty hours in connection to your 60 or 70 hour clock. Once you have reached that 60 or 70 hour limit, you have to shut down and do a *'34 hour re-set'*, which means you have to stay 'off duty' for 34 straight hours, after which you can start a new 60 or 70 hour clock. But you should discuss those techniques with your trainers. If you manage your *'On Duty'* status efficiently, you can get one additional day of driving in during your 60/70 hour work week. This means more miles and more money.

By the way, in regards to the 60 or 70 hour on-duty rule, DOT allows you to use either a 7 or 8 day calculation. In other words, no more than 60 on-duty hours in a 7 consecutive day period, or 70 on-duty hours in a 8 consecutive day period.

Note: During my research on the Department of Transportation and Federal Motor Carriers Safety Administration web sites, I noticed that the above rules pertaining to 11 hour, 14 hour, 7/8 day and 160/170 hour driving and on-duty times, is set to expire on July 1, 2013. There is no indication that new rules are being implemented, so I don't know if they are changing. Keep this in mind, as many of these rules are subject to change at any time.

One change I am aware of is a new law effective July 1, 2013, is in regards to a mandatory a break. The new regulation makes a 30 minute break mandatory after eight hours of logging 'On-Duty'.

Also, for those of you that may be hauling loads into and out of Canada, the rules are slightly different.

In regards to freight in and out of Mexico, most trucking companies will relay their trailer/ load to a Mexican trucking company, who completes the delivery into Mexico. This is due to the increased dangers of truck hijacking in Mexico among other reasons.

Keep Detailed Written Records until Proficient with Electronic Logging

When I started, the company had been using electronic logging for about a year. After struggling with the paper logs for the 4 weeks of training, I welcomed the electronic logs. But here are some suggestions. Make sure you keep a detailed written record of activity in case someone from your administrative office calls to advise you they are missing logs from you for certain dates, or are missing critical information, i.e., DVIR (Daily Vehicle Inspection Report) times, load numbers, trailer numbers associated with those load numbers etc. That happened to me twice. I really struggled to find the information they were requesting. I was not as proficient as I should have been when I first started and missed logging critical information. So, in the beginning, I recommend getting a pocket calendar or medium size spiral tablet, and recording the load number, trailer number and time you conducted your end of day DVIR (Daily Vehicle Inspection Report) as well as any other information you received in connection with each load.

Trailer Integrity Verification (TIV) Reports

In addition to your Pre-Trip and Post-Trip and DVIR Inspections, you will also be conducting 'TIV' (Trailer Integrity Verification) Reports. These are conducted in-route as you are driving. Some companies want you to do a TIV inspection within 50 miles of leaving the shipper. Some states require in-route inspections within a specific period (25 to 100 miles) when carrying hazardous material. These inspections are encouraged to help catch problems that may occur while you are en-route, before they develop into critical problems that would endanger you, the public, the trailer, and the safe delivery of the freight. This is especially critical in the hot summer months, when tires that are re-treads, tend to heat up and separate from the tire. But you are also looking for anything that will cause the integrity of the trailer to be called into question. I conducted TIV's <u>every time</u> I stopped, for whatever reason. It is always better to be cautious. Some of the things you will look for when conducting a TIV is anything that might be leaking or broken/missing, is your lock secure and is the seal on your trailer doors secure. Also look for any packages that may have been placed where it shouldn't be. Let me be blunt. You are looking for possible explosive devices or drugs that may have been placed on your truck or trailer. If you find anything that looks suspicious, back off, and call the local police. Don't try investigating something like that on your own. If it really looks suspicious, it is not worth your life to mess with.

In a more recent incident, can you imagine a pressure cooker type bomb (Boston Marathon) placed behind your cab or duct taped under your trailer. Don't assume it can't or won't happen. As recent incidents have demonstrated, there are people out there looking for ways to kill people and destroy property. Be vigilant!

As you are conducting these inspections, your engine should be off, in order to better hear for any leaks. Your lights should be on as well as your flashers and brake lights should be activated. There is a switch in your truck that activates your brake lights, and your company should show you where that is during training. Every truck is different, so be sure to ask if they don't show you.

While conducting these TIV inspections I often found things that were leaking that shouldn't be; I found tail lights that had apparently burned out since my pre-trip inspection, and headlights burned out. The tail lights are easy to take out and replace, but the headlight bulb is just a little more complicated. When you know which type of truck you will be driving, i.e., Freightliner, International, Kenworth, etc., have one of the instructors show you how to replace the headlight bulb, so you are at least familiar with how it is done. This will make it less stressful when it does happen to you. The first time it happened to me, I was really lucky to be parked in the Wal-Mart parking lot. I called our company department that deals with helping drivers with any kind of vehicle breakdown or equipment failure. The Schneider representative walked me through the process and advised me to go into Wal-Mart automotive section to see if they had a replacement. Sure enough they had a perfect replacement bulb. I got lucky.

Again, in connection with the statistics on violations listed near the end of this book, I added up all the violations that were related to the above topic of conducting good Pre/Post and TIV inspections to catch any problems early and keeping up on your Periodic Maintenance (PM). As a result of roadside inspections conducted in the U.S. only in 2012, there were 3,526,446 violations related to vehicle violations, i.e., inoperable head lights, tire tread issues, brakes out of adjustment, failure to log required inspections, oil leaks, turn signals and brake lights inoperable, defective brakes, defective windshield wipers, no fire extinguisher, audible air leaks, inadequate brakes, wheel fasteners loose, frame cracked, horn inoperative, insufficient brake linings, no spare fuses, leaking cargo, defective trailer brakes, tire rim cracked, etc. That is a HUGE number of violations! All of those violations were preventable, by simply doing their job and conducting the required inspections.

Do Not Cut Your 11/14 Hour Clock Too Close

You want to keep as much of your 60/70 hour On Duty time available for driving. You run out of time faster than you may think. I remember having an 'HOS Violation' (Hours of Service Violation) within my first month because I was so focused on driving as much as I could each day. I cut it too close and ended up unable to find parking anywhere. I ended up driving in excess of my 11 allowed hours because I did not plan ahead. I just assumed there would be some place coming up where I could park. My suggestion is to use some of your Off Duty time in the evening, prior to going to sleep, to check just how much farther you have to go, which you can get from the same device you use for your electronic logs. It will tell you exactly how much further you have to go. Also look on your map to double check any major cities you will be going through, account for morning and evening rush hour traffic. Start looking where you might be after 10 hours of driving and where would be a good place to spend the night. Before long, you will get the hang of it and will be able to do a lot of this trip planning in your head.

CHAPTER 6

WORK FLOW

Schneider National uses a system called 'work flow' to manage all the various steps or procedures required to successfully complete an assignment. I won't go into detail, because that is not the purpose of this book, and the process is constantly being updated and improved. So anything I try to share with you here will be completely out of date by the time this book is published.

No matter what 'break-in' company you end up working for, they will have some kind of work flow system for you to receive assignments and a system by which they will manage that load from pre-assignment to delivery.

The basics of any work-flow system will be the same. You will have a device in your truck that will be used to communicate with your dispatcher and company. When you are given your first pre-assignment, you will have to do your '*trip planning*' to determine if you have the time available to get the load to its destination. You will also need to provide you're *Estimated Time of Arrival* (ETA) and you're *Next Available Time (NAT)*. The load planner will not just give you another load as soon as you finish your last load. They don't know if you need time off to run an errand, if you are sick and need some time off, or if you need to do a reset because you are low on hours, etc. You need to include your *Next Available Time* (NAT) so the load planner can start looking for another load to assign you as soon as you deliver your current load. Most of the time, that should be within 30 minutes of the time you drop you current load, which is your ETA.

Learning any new system can make you feel like your head is going to explode. I know, I had a rough experience when I was trying to learn the work flow system Schneider used. I thought I would never understand it. Just remember when you are going through the orientation training, the instructors simply do not have the luxury of time. They have a lot of information and a finite period of time to relay that information. So, take the time to read and review the material two or three times <u>before</u> class so you at least have some working knowledge of the subject matter and will pick it up faster as the instructor is introducing the material.

The point I want to make here is what ever system you use, it will very confusing at first. My suggestion is to make up your own 'checklist' of steps to go through, so when you are on your own, you won't go blank and panic because you can't remember all the steps. With your checklist, laminated, there will be a lot less stress.

If your carrier uses the *Qualcomm* system in their trucks, you are lucky. This system, once you get familiar with it, has loads on information right at your finger tips that will make your trip planning easy. This system keeps a running account of how many hours you have left on your 11, 14 and 70/80 clocks, how many miles you have left to arrive at your destination, and a lot more. All this is available with the push of a couple buttons. Take advantage of this great tool and explore all the information available on this device.

CHAPTER 7

YOUR FIRST SOLO LOAD

Truck breakdowns

As you go through your initial training and orientation, take the opportunity to ask all the instructors questions during your down time. Your instructors are loaded with valuable driving experience that is not taken advantage of. Ask each of your instructors to share with you situations when their truck or trailer broke down and what they did to remedy the problem. The information they will share with you will help you be better prepared when a similar breakdown happens to you. Another good source of solutions to any kind of vehicle or mechanical breakdown is the mechanics in the various company shops. Just ask them what type repairs they had to make to trucks and trailers that easily could have been done by the driver. Those mechanics are the experts and are a good source of information and are often just taken for granted by drivers.

It is better to be prepared to address small things on your truck or trailer than simply relying on your dispatcher to solve minor problems. It will take hours for them to get someone to you to fix the problem. Meanwhile you are making NO money and burning valuable time.

Whenever you have a malfunction or problem you should advise your dispatcher. But, that does not mean that if you think you can make a repair or patch it up enough to get it to a repair facility, the dispatcher will probably advise you to go ahead. There will obviously be some circumstances where repairs are beyond your capability, at which point your dispatcher will direct you what you to do. But do your part early in your training to help prepare yourself. You do that by asking lots of questions. Questions like; how to change a headlight lamp and a trailer lamp; how to change the gears on the trailer hand crank; how to free up tandems on a trailer that won't slide, etc. If ANY question comes to mind, write it down and ask your instructors when the opportunity presents itself.

When you are prepared to address minor problems that come up now and then with your truck or the trailer, and are actually able to fix the problem yourself, there is a great sense of accomplishment.

As I mentioned before, my very first load from Denver to Salt Lake City, I hit a deer in Laramie, Wyoming. Even though the headlight was damaged, I Knew I could get to Salt Lake City before nightfall. Therefore I did not take the time to get it repaired. I got the truck to the operation center and they fixed the light.

After getting to Salt Lake and being assigned another truck, I was off to Texas for my 2nd load. On this trip my truck broke down in Santa Fe, New Mexico. This time the Turbo unit on the engine failed. The truck had little or no power to pull up any hill or incline. So after calling the department that deals with truck breakdowns, they asked me if I could make it 60 miles to the truck dealership in Albuquerque instead of waiting hours for a tow truck. I reviewed the terrain from my map and determined that there were no real hills on the 60 mile stretch of I-25, so I got the truck back on the highway and slowly made my way into Albuquerque.

Then there was the incident in a winter storm where the windshield wiper sprayer was malfunctioning, making it impossible to see out the window. I did not call my dispatcher on this malfunction. I just took a close look at the wiper and determined what the problem was, fixed it (which I discuss later) and I was back on the road within an hour. Those are just three incidents where I could have just told my dispatcher that I wanted it fixed now, but I would have lost days in the process waiting for someone to get to me.

Again, prepare yourself the best you can. Get to know your truck and the possible issues that are common for that truck as well as how to address those issues. The same holds true for the trailers your company uses.

Recommended Tools and Supplies

In connection with being prepared, it is important to make sure you have these items and tools in your truck before you hit the road on your own:

1. One large to medium size claw hammer.

When you are hooking up to an empty trailer, you need to open that trailer up to inspect the interior. You will have to sweep the trailer out. Most companies have a policy that requires you to sweep out every empty trailer you pick up. This is done because the next customer will demand that their product be placed into a clean trailer. This is especially true in the case of a food product. If the trailer is not swept out and clean, a manufacturer will often refuse to load their product until the trailer is swept out. As you sweep out the trailer you may run across nails in the floor that were used to secure wood pieces to the floor on the previous load. Often, as they removed the lumber from the floor, the nails remain and must be pulled out. Some of these nails are large and may require a large claw hammer. There are some nails that can't be pulled out, so you need to hammer them into the floor so they don't catch on pallets that are pushed into your trailer.

2.   One three pound sledge hammer with a short handle.

Sometimes you need a big hammer to bend things back in place, to straighten out DOT bumpers on trailers, to get trailer pins to retract that are stuck, etc.

3.   One large push type broom to sweep out your trailers.

This can usually be stored behind your cab, on the outside, by sliding it between the grab bar behind the cab and anything else that will help hold it in place. Every truck is different, so as you are going through your training make sure you make it a point to ask your instructor where on the truck you would secure a push broom. My instructor kept a small push broom that broke down into two pieces and fit into the side storage compartment.

4.   One 25 foot 12 gauge extension cord.

This would be used in case you need to plug your truck in during really cold weather. If the temperature falls below minus 10, companies usually want you to keep the truck idling and not plug it in. Check your company materials on winter preparation.

5.   One or two rolls of duct tape.

As you know, duct tape has a thousand uses. I used it to keep some wire in place on the Sirius Radio I installed. I also used it to repair a large gash in the side of an empty trailer I was assigned to hook up to. It is important to keep water out of the trailer to prevent your load from getting wet and possibly damaging the product. So, instead of spending an hour or two trying to find another trailer, I just patched up the one I had, filed a report regarding the damage I found and a recommendation to get it fixed. I then hit the road with my patched up trailer. I knew that operations would read my report about the gash and have the trailer taken to an operations center to have the gash repaired properly.

6.   Bolt cutter.

In case you pick up a relay from someone else and they forget to take their lock off, you will need to cut that lock off before dropping the trailer at the final destination.

7.   An assortment of open and closed ended wrenches, an adjustable wrench and some socket wrenches.

8.   An assortment of screwdrivers

9.   Assortment of regular pliers and needle nose pliers.

These last three items are useful for repairs in the cab, replacing a headlight, small wiring repairs, etc.

10.   One large 36 inch crowbar.

I used my crow bar to help loosen up the pins on the trailer tandems. They often get stuck.

11.   A good pair of Vice Grip Pliers.

Often with older trailers, the pull handle for locking pins fails to lock in place. These pull bars have a notch in them that is designed to catch on the frame and lock in the 'out' position to keep the locking pins retracted. This allows you to slide the tandems forward and back. When you pull the handle out, the locking pins retract. When you release the handle the pins snap back into the holes in the frame preventing any further movement of the rear tandem wheels. I would slide the tandems back and forth to adjust my bridge to comply with the various state bridge laws or to adjust my trailer weight. Sometimes this notch would be worn out and fail to catch on the frame to keep the handle from springing back. I would have to use my vice grip pliers to clamp down on the bar, right in front of the frame, so it prevented the bar from springing back under the trailer. This allowed me to slide the trailer tandems. Once I have the tandems where I needed them, I would release the vice grip and allow the bar/handle to spring back under the trailer, allowing the pins to reset back into the holes in the trailer frame.

12. One roll of mechanics wire.

     When duck tape won't work, mechanics wire will.

13. Various lengths of plastic ties.

     You may have to secure something or hold it in place.

14. A good bright flashlight.

     Interstate Batteries' sells some great handheld lights.

15. Two pairs of work gloves.

     They will get dirty fast. I address gloves elsewhere in this book.

16. Glad Hand grommets.

     Just ask your mechanic or operations desk. I cover this item later on in another chapter.

17. Trailer stop lights, beehive marker lights, side marker lights and interior cab light bulbs.

     They often go out and are easy to replace. The trailer lights are held in by a rubber gasket. They are simple to remove, unplug, then plug in new one and push it back into the rubber gasket. If the shop will give you a spare headlight lamp, get that as well.

18. Two padlocks for your trailer door.

     I recommend having two padlocks available. On occasion, you may drop a trailer and forget to take you lock off. Then you are left with no lock for your next load. I did this 3 times. So, try to discipline yourself to always take your lock off when you stop at the gate of your destination.

The operations desk will only give you one lock. Just visit a different operations center and tell them you accidently left your lock on a trailer. Now you have a spare lock.

19. Load straps/bars.

Sometimes the shipper may require you to secure the load. So be prepared. You can pick these up at your operations desk. Practice using them inside an empty trailer so you are familiar with how they secure to the slots inside the trailer and how the strap pulls tight. The load bars simply are applied to the inside ribs of the trailer and expanded. Review your company material for more detail on securing a load.

20. Hard hat, safety glasses and safety vest.

Many shippers will not allow you on their property without them.

21. Two cans of WD-40.

Sometimes the pins on the tandems are really difficult to operate due to age and corrosion. Just soak it down with WD-40, wait 10 minutes and try again. This product can also be needed during really cold weather to help prevent your fifth wheel from malfunctioning. I go into this more later.

There will be numerous additional items your company will want you to have in your truck, like company paperwork, logs, manifest forms, labels, etc. All that should be covered in your training.

Backing Your Trailer

The most important thing to remember as you start out on your first Solo run is to SLOW DOWN and take your time. Make sure you go through all your steps as instructed. There is NO rush. You WILL get frustrated because you will feel like you are taking forever to get things done. You will worry that you are forgetting something. Things will not always go your way. But just be aware, it is at times like these that mistakes are made and your focus goes out the window. The next thing you know, you have hit something with either your trailer or your truck. Again, slow down! I know it is difficult to do, but you have to force yourself to stop, refocus, take a few deep breaths, get out of the truck and take the time to assess your situation, then, go slow.

While you are going through your training, there is a reason the instructors tell you to 'get out and look', as many time as you need to while backing a trailer into any space. In regards to your blind spot, you simply cannot see exactly where the rear of your trailer is. When backing a trailer into any space, try to back in so you can see your space from your driver window, and see exactly where the driver side of your trailer is. You get out so you can see where the blind side (right side) of your trailer is going. This applies to any ally dock parking maneuver.

To illustrate this point, let me relate a story of an accident I witnessed. I was backed into a dock waiting for this warehouse to finish loading my trailer. I had trucks & trailers on both sides of me, which were also being loaded. This is a very busy distributor, with trucks coming and going 24 hours a day. The truck and trailer two spaces to my left was finished being loaded and pulled out. There was another truck and trailer waiting to pull into this space. I could tell right away, as this driver was positioning his trailer to back into this dock, that something was wrong. He did not pull forward enough to give him sufficient room to maneuver his trailer into the space. As he was backing in he was coming in at a very shallow angle and it was clear he was going to hit the truck parked next to me. While watching this, I and the truck to my right, who was also watching this, began to pull on our air horns to warn the driver to stop. He did not stop and ended taking out the side of the truck parked next to me.

What was even worse, once he hit the truck, he <u>didn't stop</u>! He continued to push the trailer further down the truck until people started to yell at him to stop. The driver pulled forward a few feet<u>, never got out of his truck</u>, and started to back right back into the same truck, <u>again</u>!

This driver turned out to be a new driver, but who obviously had very poor training in safely backing his trailer. Part of me felt sorry for the guy, and part of me was angry with whatever school and licensing system and carrier that would allow someone who was so poorly trained, to be out there on the road.

My very first load was at a paper company in Denver. This company had an extremely small docking area. In addition, they had empty trailers parked along the fence making it almost impossible to back into their docks. Once I dropped my empty trailer and hooked into my loaded trailer at the dock, there was not enough room to pull out of the dock without hitting the trailer parked right next to me. So I had to pull out the other direction, hoping I had room at the end of the docking area to turn around. Well, there was no room to turn around. I got really frustrated, lost my focus and came within ½ inch of scraping the side of another trailer due to the tight conditions and my inexperience with maneuvering in really tight spaces. It took me 2 hours from beginning to end before I got the load on the road. While picking up my paper work from the clerk after finally getting positioned to leave the premises with my load, I apologized for taking so long to get the trailer out. The clerk advised me, "Don't feel bad, I have seen a lot worse. I have seen drivers take 4 hours". He told me some drivers simply drive away in frustration, leaving without their assigned load. Those comments made me feel a little better.

Coupling & Uncoupling

By the way, in regards to coupling and uncoupling trailers. During your orientation you will receive some training and tips on how to do it safely. <u>Pay attention</u>. They usually want you to follow specific steps, in a specific order, in a systematic manner. They do this for a reason. Based on their experience, if you follow the steps they outline, in order, and perform them with due diligence, you will mitigate any serious problems while performing these functions. I will not cover all the critical steps (their all critical) but only those that I had problems with and learned to pay better attention to.

While you are practicing with the instructors, they are watching for any mistakes and will (hopefully) stop you before you accidently drop a trailer on the ground or bend the locking handle, etc. There are some points I would like to emphasis that I found were critical once you are out there on your own, without anyone there to save you from mental errors that may cost you your life or job.

First, let's address coupling or hooking the truck up to a trailer.

As you back into the trailer you are trying to hook up to and your rear wheels begin to go under the nose of the trailer, STOP. Set the parking brake, put the truck in neutral and get out of the truck to eyeball exactly where the nose of the trailer will be making contact with your 5th wheel. The back of your fifth wheel should be tilted down toward the trailer. The trailer should make contact with the fifth wheel no closer than 11 inches from the fifth wheel pivot point (where the 5th wheel pivots down toward the trailer). If the trailer is too high, then take the time to lower the trailer. I know this is a lot of work, and it is sometimes very difficult, but if you don't, and the trailer is too high, you run a BIG risk of not coupling correctly or running the king pin right over the 5th wheel and getting it stuck in front of the fifth wheel.

I came very close to doing just that on one occasion. I failed to get out and look exactly where the trailer nose was making contact because I was in a hurry. As I was backing under the trailer, something just didn't feel right, so I immediately stopped. I got out to take a look and sure enough, the king pin was riding on top of the fifth wheel, and within 3 inches of dropping down in front of the fifth wheel. If that happens, you will then need a fork lift or something similar to lift the trailer up so you can get out from under it without damaging the 5th wheel, king pin or the 5th wheel release handle. You may be able to use the crank handle to raise the trailer as high as it will go thereby possibly giving you enough room to maneuver out from under the trailer without causing any damage. But don't count on it. The landing gear may not extend enough to allow the king pin to get high enough to clear the 5th wheel. I have seen other drivers in this situation use large pieces of lumber to place under the landing gear, and then crank the landing gear down to raise the trailer enough to pull the truck forward.

The point here is to avoid this situation in the first place by taking the time to get out and look to insure the last driver to drop this trailer did not leave it sitting so high that the king pin goes right over the fifth wheel, or is too high to properly lock into the 5th wheel.

To say the least this would have really messed up my day and would have been extremely embarrassing, not to mention it may have cost me my job.

I slowly pulled the truck forward until my rear wheels were just under the trailer, with the nose of the trailer about 11 inches from the pivot point of the fifth wheel. I then got out, and lowered the trailer with the hand crank until the nose of the trailer was actually resting slightly on the back part of the fifth wheel, causing it to tilt down. I could actually see the mud flaps on the rear wheels of the truck dip down due to the weight of the trailer on the 5th wheel. I made sure the king pin was centered correctly and then backed under the trailer so I actually <u>picked up</u> the trailer with the back portion of my fifth wheel, insuring the king pin would properly engage and lock into the fifth wheel.

As a side note, keep your 5th wheel well greased. Every time you happen to be at one of your company operating centers, have the personnel or mechanics apply some grease to your fifth wheel.

Mexico & Rubber Grommets

Another embarrassing mistake I made while picking up a trailer in Laredo, Texas, during a hot humid summer day. I was warned in advance to be sure to check the rubber grommets that are fastened to the face of the trailer air hose. Often trailers that have come back to the U.S. from Mexico are missing their rubber grommets, which allow for a good seal between the truck glad hands and the trailer, preventing air leaks. Apparently the grommets are stolen by the kids in Mexico, for whatever reason. When the Mexican drivers have to replace the grommets so they can get the trailer back to the U.S., they then remove them once the trailer is dropped back in the U.S. Without those grommets, the air lines cannot make a good seal, and you cannot move the trailer.

I was attempting to attach the truck air hoses to the trailer I was assigned to pick up, but was unable to get the glad hands to fasten correctly to prevent air from escaping. I called the mechanic because I was unable to figure out what the malfunction was. He checked it and told me there were no grommets on the trailer *Glad Hands*. I had one of those embarrassing moments when you failed to see what was right before your eyes. Like when you are looking high and low for something in the house, and yell at your wife for hiding it somewhere. Then she walks into the room, points to the counter, and just laying there, right before your eyes, was the item you were so desperately looking for. You wife then glares at you and says "If it were a snake it would have bitten you".

I was so embarrassed; I just closed my eyes, looked down and started shaking my head. I was so hot and tired; I simply failed to see what was right before me. I even carry extra grommets just for this occasion, so it's not like I wasn't prepared. I never made that mistake again.

Uncoupling or dropping your trailer is easier, but there are real critical steps you must take in order to prevent dropping the trailer on the ground because you failed to lower the landing gear, or you tear out your air houses and electrical lines because you forgot to disconnect them. I again go back to the beginning of this section when I advised following the steps exactly, just as your employer trains you.

I had one instance where I came within inches of dropping my full trailer on the ground. I was in Texas, it was summer, it was hot, humid and dusty. It was pure hell. I had been waiting 2 days for a load. Other drivers I spoke with said they hated bringing loads to Laredo, Texas, because there are not enough loads out of Laredo. So you just have to wait in line for your turn. Anyway, I was very eager to get out of there. I finally got a load, had hooked up to it and was ready to go. While trying to exit the yard, I was advised that U.S. Customs had not cleared the trailer yet. So I had to back up, and put the trailer back. Later I was advised that the trailer had been cleared. But when I tried to exit, I was again advised the trailer still had not been cleared by customs. This on again, off again went on for a couple hours. I was tired, hot and angry. Finally, I was told to go ahead and pick up the same trailer, again. In the middle of my 'steps' to pick the trailer back up again, my dispatcher called me, apologized and advised me to just put the trailer back because Customs still had not cleared the load. He had a different load for me. Because I had been distracted in the middle of all this, I failed to check if I had done everything necessary to drop the trailer safely. As I started to pull out from under the trailer, I had this gut feeling that something was wrong. So I immediately stopped, put the brakes on and jumped out to double check everything. I noticed I had failed to put down the landing gear, and was just 6 inches from dropping a fully loaded trailer on the ground. I felt sick! I immediately put down the landing gear and then completed my uncoupling check list.

I have heard stories from other drivers and instructors that have actually dropped trailers because they got distracted by someone coming over to them to ask a question or ask for help. They then failed to double check their uncoupling checklist, and ended up dropping the trailer on the ground. If this happens to you, that is, you get distracted for any reason; make it a personal policy to start over from the beginning of your check list for both coupling and uncoupling. When you make a mistake in this industry, it can be costly.

In some trucks, when uncoupling from a loaded trailer, there will be enough air in your air bags to reduce traction on the rear drive axel. The rear drive wheels will spin, preventing you from driving away. In this case either wait 30 to 60 seconds to allow the air bags to adjust before driving away, or before pulling out from under the trailer, engage your power divider, which engages both axels, and allows you to pull out without waiting. After pulling out, make sure the tires are NOT spinning when you unlock the power divider. Again, DO NOT unlock the power divider if the rear axle drive is spinning. You can seriously damage the gears in power divider.

Scales, Bridge Laws & Weight Distribution

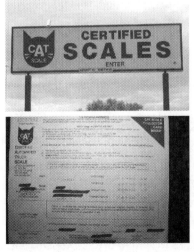

Most companies want you to scale or weigh every load. Since most companies will pay the cost of scaling a load, there is no excuse for not doing it. Some shippers will have scales on site, so ask. Otherwise you will need to go to a CAT scale, which are located at a number of the truck stop locations. Make sure you have your trainer show you how to do this so you are not completely confused when you have to do it by yourself on your first solo load.

You will need to grab your permit book that is in your truck, usually located in the driver's side door pocket. Check the bridge laws for each state you will be traveling through. You must scale your load/ adjust your bridge/ tandems, for all the states you will be traveling through as well as your destination state. Scale all loads over 30,000 lbs. as soon as possible after the load has been picked up so you can address problems early. You do not want to find out you are overweight while going through a weigh station and get a ticket. On top of the ticket, you now cannot go any further until the overweight issue is taken care of. Even relay loads that you pick up from another driver should be scaled. The invoice from the shipper usually will have a good estimated weight to help you determine if the load is over 30,000 lbs., and should be scaled.

Bridge laws were a mystery to me as I was going through training. I just could not figure out why they exist, so I asked an instructor. Some states, particularly the eastern states, have some roads that are very old and were not built to accommodate the length of a big truck with a fifty-three foot trailer. So some states have established maximum distances between the king pin of the trailer and the center of the rear tandems. Manufacturers and shippers who are sending loads to these more restrictive states will load the trailer heavy in the nose/front of the trailer, making it easier to balance the weight between the axels.

Again, make sure you check your bridge/kingpin settings for each state you will go through. Set your bridge/kingpin distances for the most restrictive state you will be going through. You will learn more about these bridge/kingpin settings, and sliding the rear tandems while you go through training.

I recommend that as you go through your initial driver training for your Commercial Drivers License, there will often be a lot of down time. Grab an instructor and ask him to show you how to adjust the rear tandem wheels and fifth wheel and under what circumstances you would make those adjustments. They will be happy to share their knowledge with you. Basically, you are limited on the amount of weight each axel can carry. The standard weight limits are:

12,000 lbs. for the steer axel, 34,000 lbs for the drive axels, and 34,000 lbs. for the trailer axels. The Gross Vehicle Combined Weight cannot exceed 80,000 lbs.

Basically, think of a teeter-totter in a playground. The center is the perfect balance point. If you are carrying too much weight on your drive axels, say 36,000 lbs, and only 30,000 lbs. on your trailer axels, simply sliding the rear tandem axels forward, toward the front of the trailer, three or four slots, should balance the load. As you move the rear axels towards the front of the trailer, the weight begins to shift to the rear/trailer axels.

In the opposite scenario when you have too much weight on the trailer axels, slide the rear tandems toward the rear of the trailer to shift the weight to the drive axles.

On most CAT certified truck scales, they will weight each axel independently. When approaching a truck stop, simply identify where the scale is located. Make sure you are pulling into the scale from the correct direction. Pull all the way up to the 'talk box' that will be right at window height. Reach out and push the button. The attendant at the fuel desk inside the truck stop will ask you, "First weigh or re-weigh"; you will tell them this is your first weigh. They will then ask for your truck and trailer number, so have those ready. About 15-30 seconds later they will tell you to go ahead and pull off the scale and come inside for your ticket.

Do not park on the scale or in front of the scale, as other drivers will be coming through to scale their loads. Pull off the scales and either find a legal parking spot somewhere on the lot, or pull up to the fueling islands and get fuel if needed. Then pull up just like all the other trucks are doing, leaving room for trucks behind you to pull up and fuel their trucks. Park it right there, put your brakes on, take your keys, lock your truck up and go into building to the fuel desk to pay for your scale. You have just enough time to pay for your scale, go to the restroom, and grab a drink before you need to get back to your truck to allow the truck behind you that just finished fueling, to pull up into the your spot.

The fuel desk generally will not advise you of any weight problems until you come inside to pay for and pick up your scale receipt. If there are problems with the load, use your training to adjust the weight. If you are overweight (80,000 lbs.) you will need to call your dispatcher and request further instructions. Generally this will mean a trip back to the shipper to have some of the product removed. This is why it is important to scale your load as early in the process as possible.

Most shippers know exactly how much of their product they can load onto a trailer, so there is rarely a problem. I have only come close to 80,000 lbs. on one occasion. It was a load of salt that put me within 200 lbs. of maximum. If you are just barely overweight you may be able to mitigate the problem by running your fuel tanks down to half full and keep them there. Talk with your instructor about this issue and see what they recommend.

Returning To Truck after Fueling

After you have completed your business inside the truck stop and you are walking back to your truck, you <u>must</u> make the assumption that someone may have tampered with your truck while you were inside. Do a quick visual inspection of the following items on your truck:

1. Make sure the lock and seal on your trailer doors are still intact and secure.
2. Make sure your tail lights and head lights are still intact and not broken.
3. Check ALL tires for the type of damage that would suggest they were slashed.
4. Check that the lever used to pull the pins from the tandems on the trailer has not been tampered with and that all four pins are still in place.
5. Make sure your landing gear is up and the handle is secured.
6. MOST IMPORTANTLY, get under the trailer (Engine OFF) and make sure the locking mechanism is still securely fastened

around the king pin, or the locking bar is all the way across the king pin. Check the locking handle to insure it is all the way in. Unfortunately, there are idiots out there who think it is funny to pull the locking handle on your fifth wheel while you are in the truck stop. This basically unlocks the king pin, so that when you pull out, your trailer separates and drops to the ground. The trailer may not separate right away. It may not separate until you are back on the freeway. This is very dangerous to other drivers near your trailer, can damage your cargo and damage the trailer. Not to mention, now you have to get a tow truck to lift your trailer so you can get back under it. I have talked to drivers who this has happened to and in the case of an empty trailer, they were able to put their landing gear in low gear and crank it, allowing the landing gear to lift the trailer until they could get the truck back under the trailer. If your trailer is full, using the landing gear may not be an option. The point here is to avoid the accident all together by taking a couple minutes to double check these items before you climb back into your cab.

CHAPTER 8

TRUCK STOPS

There are five major truck stops, 'Pilot', 'Flying J', 'Loves', 'TA Travel Centers' and 'Petro Travel Centers'.

Rewards/ Loyalty Cards

Make a point to visit each of these Truck Stops / Travel Centers as soon as possible and sign up for the rewards program at each one. This allows you to begin to build up points for free food, coffee or any merchandise they sell at any of their respective locations. These five major companies have truck stops in just about every state.

So, when you use the company credit card to pay for your company truck's fuel, were talking hundreds of dollars to fill the tanks on both sides of the truck, you can build up points really fast!

After you swipe your company credit card, it will usually ask you to swipe your rewards card. Have your truck number, employee ID number, current mileage, and in some states your truck license plate number, ready to punch into the fuel dispenser keyboard.

Free Company Directory Guides

In addition, make sure you pick up the latest little free book at all the above five major truck stops, which lists all the most recent locations that particular company has in each state. The book gives you each state, and specific directions, name of highway and exit numbers where each truck stop is located. When you know where you are going with your load, it should be part of your trip planning process to see which of these major truck stops are on the routes you will be traveling. These are a valuable resource and their free. There is also the National Truck Stop Directory, which is about the size of your Truckers Road Atlas, and contains all the truck stops in USA and Canada. You have to pay around $20.00 for one of these, but it is well worth the price.

Free Ice

One unexpected bonus that I never failed to get was free ice for my small cooler that I kept my drinks in, right next to my seat. It only would hold about four cans or bottles. Whenever I went inside the truck stop, I would ask the clerk if I could put a little ice from the soda dispenser into my plastic bag for my small cooler. I never had anyone say no. Since it is only about five cups of ice, they usually have no problem with it. Just make sure you bring your own bag. I usually make a purchase just before I ask. So just keep that in mind when you may need a little ice.

Free Showers

You also earn credits for free showers with your rewards card, which is a real valuable benefit, since showers cost at least $10.00 if you had to pay for them.

You can earn a shower approximately every time you fill your fuel tanks. Those shower credits do expire about 10 days after they are earned, so make sure you keep up on how many credits you have on each of your reward cards. If you have a shower about to expire at a particular truck stop, you may want to make it a point to visit or stay at this truck stop soon.

I have learned that Loves Truck Stops had the best overall shower facilities, but, Pilot and Flying J truck stops are in the process of upgrading theirs. The company you work for may restrict where you are authorized to fuel your truck. They often get favorable fuel contracts with specific companies.

Company Fueling Recommendations

Also be aware that when you accept a load, and they give you specific re-fueling 'suggestions' along the route they provide, follow those 'suggestions'. If you re-fuel at locations other than what they suggest, it will jeopardize your chances of qualifying for your quarterly bonus. It sounds rather ridiculous, but the program they use to plot your route also has information on where the cheapest fuel prices are. Sometimes it can be very frustrating. For example, on one occasion I picked up a load in Las Vegas to be delivered in Los Angeles. My routing instructions sent me 18 miles northeast out of Las Vegas to fuel at a Love's Truck Stop, when I was literally a stone's throw from a Pilot Truck Stop. After fueling at the Love's, I had to drive back to Las Vegas and on to Los Angeles. That whole detour ate up almost 2 hours of my time just so they could save a couple cents a gallon. Even though I got almost sixty gallons of fuel and saved them $10.00, it was a real waste of my time. So just be aware of why they send you to specific truck stops to re-fuel and that following those re-fueling 'suggestions' is part of the formula the company uses to determine if you qualify for your quarterly bonus.

Getting a Good Nights Sleep

I was fortunate while doing my 'on the road' training to make at least seven trips involving maneuvering, parking and sleeping at trucking stops. My trainer advised me to get to the truck stop as early as you can to get a good spot. Avoid parking next to Refrigerated trailers as they run all night and can interfere with getting a good night's sleep. Also, invest in some really soft ear plugs. I wore earplugs every night, regardless of where I stayed. I always got good night's sleep. You can create the conditions in your sleeper which make it perfect for getting a good night's sleep. You can make it really dark, by pulling the windshield curtains as well as the curtains that separate the sleeper from the front seats. You have no distractions such as pets and family members and all the distractions you can think of that may disturb your sleep while at home. Put your soft earplugs completely into your ears, so they don't fall out. You now have perfect conditions for getting the sleep you need to be rested and alert the next morning. I have never slept as well as I have in the truck. Sounds weird I know, but if you take the right steps, you should rarely have a bad night. Driving when you are tired is a receipt for disaster.

Where to Sleep?

Once I was on my own, I quickly found out that getting to a truck stop early is only possible if you start your day really early. That is not always possible due to restrictions in getting at least 10 hours rest, delays in picking up your load and so forth.

What I finally learned is that when I do my trip planning the night before, I look on my map to determine approximately where I will be near the end of the day, and look for not only major cities with truck stops, but I also use my Garmin Navigator to select other areas I could spend the night. This includes rest areas, Home Depot, Lowes, Costco and Wal-Mart parking lots.

What you want to avoid is get down to less than one hour on your drive clock and not having a clue where you are going to stop. That can lead to DOT time violations as you rush around looking for a legal place to park.

Port-a-Potty

Also, consider the fact that you WILL need bathroom facilities, so keep that in mind. I purchased a porta-potty for the truck for those emergencies that sometimes happen when you are unable to find a restroom or there is simply no time. I found it on line. It is simply a 5 gallon bucket with a seat on it and special plastic liners. I am REALLY thankful I had it on two occasions where I needed to go #2 immediately! I had just enough time to pull over and pull out the 'bucket'. Sometimes when you get up in the morning, drink some water, your body immediately needs to relief itself. So, prepare for those types of circumstances. You will be really glad you did.

TransFlo Documents (FAX)

When you pull into a truck stop to fuel, try to get as much accomplished as you can to mitigate additional time wasting stops. Get any additional snacks and coffee you will need for the road. This includes the *transflo* of any paperwork from your last load. Let me explain *transflo* in more detail.

In order to get paid for each load you deliver, you need to send in the *Bill of Lading* with a '*Trip Sheet*' cover. The *Bill of Lading* usually consists of one to three pages. Every truck stop has a '*TransFlo*' machine (Like a FAX machine), the use of which is free. You can use the *TransFlo* machine to send the *Bill of Lading* to your company. Each company has their own cover sheet coded specifically for that company, called a '*Trip Sheet*' which is sent with the *Bill of Lading*. Since the trip sheet is a 'cover sheet' and is coded for your company, it is the first document fed in to the *TransFlo* machine, since it tells the machine which company to send it to. Then your Bill of Lading documents follow.

Try to *TransFlo* the *Bill of Lading* ASAP or as soon as you can. You don't get paid until your company has proof that the load was delivered. I have seen some drivers with a stack of paper work 2 inches high because they did not take the time to *TransFlo* the paperwork to their company at least every other day. This one guy I saw must have waited a month to send in all his paper work.

Warning: If you wait too long, you risk the chance of losing some of your paper work, which would be a bad situation.

CHAPTER 9

REST AREAS

Most states have spent millions of dollars developing and building first class rest stops along the major highways that run through their states. From what I saw while driving, I believe Texas has the cleanest and best designed truck stops.

These 'Rest Areas' have one side designed for passenger vehicles and one side designed specifically for trucks. So pull in to a truck stop slowly to make sure you pull into the correct area.

Parking in a Rest Stop

When pulling into a rest stop, the rest stops may have parallel parking along both curb sides or angled slot parking, both shown in the photos above.

In the case of curb side parallel parking, try to pull all the way up to allow trucks behind you to do the same. Sometimes you have no choice but to parallel park your rig between two other rigs. So make sure you practice this type of parking while in driving school and get it down on both driver side and blind side.

In regards to the angled slot parking, be careful as you pull into an empty space between two big rigs. It is easy to hit the trailer next to you with your trailer if you are not paying attention. You are usually tired as you pull into these rest stops and may cut in too early, causing your trailer to hit one of the trailers already parked. If you can, it is best to pull into a space that gives you lots of room to maneuver.

Pull into the truck stop slowly and look ahead to see if there are any spots where there are least two empty lanes next to each other. That will give you some extra maneuvering room. Most of the time you will not be able to pull in and get your truck and trailer perfectly lined up between the lines on the first try. It is best to pull forward in your space as far as you can, while maneuvering your truck and trailer between the lines. Then you can back up as you straighten out your trailer as needed. As you are backing and maneuvering, be aware that other trucks are coming in as well, so don't blindly back into their path. Take it slow so you give those trucks you can't see time to slow down or stop to allow you to maneuver your truck in your space.

Not all rest stops allow trucks, but they will usually advise truckers on some highway sign before you try entering. Oregon seems to have a lot of these 'No Trucks Allowed' rest stops.

Rest Stops vs. Truck Stops

I have come to prefer taking my mandatory 10 hour break at these rest stops as opposed to truck stops. Truck stops fill up fast and for the most part are not as clean or safe as rest stops. So, unless you need the facilities at the truck stop, i.e., restaurant, showers, fuel, supplies etc., I would try to stay at rest stops.

All the rest stops I utilized had restrooms open 24 hours. For me, that was all I needed. I had my own food supply in the truck to save money and carried two 5 gallon water containers. Often the water at these rest stops is not safe for drinking, and they will put notices up near the sinks telling you that.

By the way, Costco is a great place to stock up on healthy snacks, nuts, candy bars and whatever you need at a best 'per-unit' price.

CHAPTER 10

COMPANY OPERATING CENTERS

Most of the major trucking companies have their own National Operating Centers, scattered around the country, for their drivers to use. One of them will probably be assigned as your permanent home base. This will probably be where your dispatcher will be headquartered as well. You will return to your home operating center for evaluations and most of your post-hiring training. Most of these operating centers are fairly comprehensive. Use them whenever you can.

My home operating center was Salt Lake City. It was a smaller operating center so it did not have all of the amenities of some of the larger operating centers.

Good Place to Practice Your Parking Techniques

My favorite operating centers were French Camp and Fontana, both in California. The French Camp (Stockton) operating center was perfect for new drivers who want a lot of space to practice their alley dock parking techniques. I remember spending at least an hour practicing my parking and alley docking techniques every time I went there. I would go way in the back of the lot where I could practice without other drivers watching me. The Laredo, Texas operating center also had lots of room for a new driver to practice his parking techniques in relative privacy.

Free Showers, Washers & Dryers, etc.

Most of these operating centers have lots of parking available, free showers, free washer and dryers, ATM's, vending machines, free ice machines, free shuttles to local motels, FAX services, TransFlo machines, Free Wi-Fi for your computer, microwaves, exercise rooms and lounges where you can watch TV all night if you want. Some have pretty good cafeterias with decent food. They also have mechanics to service your truck.

These company operating centers are also very safe and quiet. Be sure to park as close to the operating center as you can so you don't have that far to walk. You will find yourself making several trips to the operating center to eat, do your laundry, use the restroom facilities, take a shower and watch the big game on the TV. So, the closer you park the more convenient it is and less of a hassle, especially if it is raining, cold and snowy or really hot.

Laundry Tips

Let me pass on a useful bit of information when it comes to doing your laundry in one of these centers or at some truck stop. If I knew I was going to be at or near an operating center in the near future, I would wait to do my laundry there, because . . . well . . . it's free and much safer than a truck stop. I use to have these quart bottles of laundry detergent and bleach I would have to lug with me every time I did laundry. They were a hassle to carry, and took up valuable space in the truck. Once my detergent leaked all over the floor of the cabinet it was stored in. I found out the lid was not on tight enough, and when it fell over, it slowly started to leak. I was lucky the container was only ¼ full.

I recently found were these little detergent 'PODS' that Tide makes. They are the size of a real small 'hacky sack'. These are small liquid, single use 'PODS' encased in clear, dissolvable plastic. They contain the right amount of detergent along with a little stain remover and brightener, in one small packet that fits right in your pocket. They are really convenient and a great space saver in the truck.

If you like to use bleach with all your whites, I recommend getting rid of the big plastic bottle of bleach and getting EVOLVE ULTRA concentrated bleach tablets. They are packaged in a small container similar to how some multi-vitamins would be packaged. It only takes one tablet per load. These really are concentrated, so be careful not to use more than one.

Whereas the POD's can be thrown in with the clothes, DO NOT put the bleach tablet in with the clothes. Put the tablet in the detergent compartment on top of the washer where the detergent usually goes. As the water flows through this compartment, it will begin to dissolve the bleach tablet. The tablet will be held in place by the plastic screen that these compartments usually have. When I first used these bleach tablets,

I just threw it in along with the POD. Well, the bleach tablet was sitting right on my t-shirt, and when it got wet from the water pouring in, the concentrated bleach ended up burning a hole in my t-shirt. The bleach had not been allowed to dilute until the washer finished filling with water and the washing cycle started. So for 3 to 4 minutes, my t-shirt got the all the bleach full strength. Lesson learned!

CHAPTER 11

SLEEPING IN TRUCK/ SLEEPING BERTH

If you set up your sleeping berth correctly, it can be just like a great mini-apartment.

Setting Up Your Mini-Apartment

Start with some memory foam to put on top of the truck mattress. Unless the truck is brand new or the mattress in the truck is brand new, someone else slept on that mattress. I highly recommend cleaning and disinfecting the mattress as much as possible. Then purchase one of those bed bug, dust mite and allergen proof mattress covers. You don't know how clean or dirty the person was who slept on that mattress before you. I would be cautious if I were you. I learned my lesson at my first duty station when I was in the Air Force.

I got a memory foam pad for a double bed from Costco, folded it in half, and placed it on top of the mattress, under my own personal mattress pad. I placed the folded part of the memory foam pad on the outside edge of the mattress, toward the front of the truck. This helped keep me in the center of the bed no matter how much I moved around at night.

Then make sure you have a pillow that you are really comfortable with. Have at least two additional pillows, one to put between your knees if you sleep on your side and one to place in the gap between your bed and the side of the truck.

If you sleep on your side, a pillow between your legs keeps your hips from twisting and slipping. This helps prevent your body from angling over as you sleep. The pillow between your legs aligns your spine and puts you in a better sleeping position. 1

I also kept a very warm sleeping bag near my head area to use if I wanted to sit up to read a book, watch movies on my computer or read my e-mail. The sleeping bag is also used in winter if I get stuck in a storm and have trouble keeping the cab warm. That sleeping bag, combined with the other blankets I normally have came in VERY handy when my cab gets really cold. There were a couple of times when the temperature dropped suddenly and unexpectedly during the night in the mountains west of Utah and in Washington State.

As far as sheets go, use flannel sheets in the winter and the cooler plain cotton sheets in the summer. They are easier to wash than a sleeping bag. The washers at most of these truck stops are small and will not accommodate a sleeping bag. Sleeping on sheets with a blanket is much more comfortable than a sleeping bag any way.

As you lay in your sleeping berth for the first time, think about what you might need during the night. While lying on your bunk, reading or using your computer, make mental notes of what you would like to have within reach, without having to get out of bed.

Using Adhesive Hooks

There are all kinds of self adhesive hooks that you can put up to hang things like power cords and earphones for your computer. It is much more convenient to have these items available, easily within reach while you are in your bunk, as opposed to having to get up to find your computer bag or search through cabinets to find those item you use every night.

When you hang up power cords, ear buds, etc., be aware that as you drive, the vibration and movement of the truck will cause these items to slide off the hook. You will need to hang them in such a manner that it will mitigate that problem.

Flashlight Placement

Think about where you would put a flashlight that you can get to quickly in case of an emergency. I had one occasion when I was awoken suddenly in the middle of the night. The truck and trailer violently rocked and scared the hell out of me. I thought I had been hit by another truck. So, I jumped out of bed, hit my head on the upper bunk, which really hurt, stumbled around, could not find my flashlight or even remember where I had it. It took me a good 5 minutes to finally get the bunk lights on, find a flashlight, get dressed and get out of the truck to find it was nothing more than a really strong cross wind that rocked the trailer and cab.

So, plan ahead. Know exactly where all the light switches are in your truck and <u>practice</u> finding those switches at night, so it will be easier to find if you are woken up from a dead sleep. You can also use one of those half dome lights you turn on by just pushing it. Just make sure you test it every once in awhile to insure the batteries are good, as they tend to go through batteries quickly. Then put it up somewhere you can reach immediately if you are suddenly woken up. The key is to know exactly <u>what</u> you are going to do if something happens that requires you to get up quickly and get outside.

I also kept one of those really powerful 2 million candle power, rechargeable, handheld flashlight to take outside if I needed to check something around the truck. It is really nice to have something that powerful to light up the area. It made me feel safer and nothing escaped that 2 million candle beam of light.

I used those self adhesive hooks to hang up my computer power cord, ear buds and cell phone recharger right near the top part of my bed area, so I could reach them easily without having to get out of bed to search some drawer to find them. I also used door hooks to hang clothe bags off the edge of the upper bunk, to store apples, oranges, bananas, etc.

Top Bunk

If you use the top bunk to place your suit case or any luggage or cargo, <u>be sure</u> to use the cargo netting to strap down whatever you put up there. Twice I forgot to secure my suitcase and while making a quick stop, my luggage fell off the upper bunk, hit my right shoulder, and almost hit the gear shift. It also spilled cloths all over the cab because I had failed to close it. Just discipline yourself to strap it back down every time you take something out of your luggage.

Windshield and Bunk Curtains

When you sleep at night, use both the windshield curtain as well as the bunk curtain behind the truck seats. This helps screen out noise and more importantly, light. Keep your sleeping area as dark as you can make it. Any outside light from passing trucks or street lights can disturb your sleep and interfere with the quality of sleep you need.

As I had mentioned previously, I set up my sleeping area so it was as dark as I could get it. While sleeping in my truck I have had some of the best nights of uninterrupted sleep ever. I typically slept much better in my truck than I did at home.

Note: You may notice that as you try to pull the two curtains into place, they often hang up and get stuck. An easy way to completely eliminate that problem and to make those curtains slide smoothly, is to step up on the seat and spray some WD-40 <u>into the aluminum tracks</u>. Use a can that has a long extendable thin straw type nozzle. Spray <u>a little</u> into the tracks every 6 inches. Keep a few paper towels handy to reach up and wipe away any drips before they land on the seats or floor. Do this to both the windshield curtain and the bunk curtain. You will be amazed how easily they glide after you apply the WD-40.

Ear Plugs

I would also use soft ear plugs to block out 90% of the outside noise from refrigerated trucks parked next to me, other trucks coming and going as well as loud conversations and the sounds of thunder storms, etc.

When you use those soft foam ear plugs, don't forget to wash them every 3 or 4 days. Just wash them with any hand soap, then rinse them, and squeeze the water out several times until you no longer get any suds when you squeeze the water out. Break out a new pair whenever you feel the old ear plugs need replacing. At night, I will always put a little water on the ear plugs to make them softer. If you buy the harder foam ear plugs, they will eventually begin to hurt your skin just inside your ear. So stick with the really soft foam. You can also go to your doctor and get ear plugs made specifically for your ears.

The bottom line is I found that you can get <u>very</u> comfortable in your truck if you set it up right.

Melatonin

I also take a product called Schiff Melatonin Ultra sleep aid. It is basically a drug free product that contains melatonin, vitamins and herbs to help you sleep more soundly throughout the night. I swear by this stuff. It really helps me go to sleep and stay asleep. I take it about one hour before I actually go to bed.

Melatonin is a hormone made by the Pineal gland which is located in the brain. Melatonin helps control your sleep and wake cycles. It is released at night or when it is dark and basically instructs the body that it is time to sleep. The level of melatonin produced declines as we get older, which is why older people tend to have difficulty sleeping. Light affects how much melatonin your body produces. This is why I recommend keeping both your windshield curtains <u>and</u> your bunk curtains closed when you go to bed. You don't want any light, i.e., headlights, street lights etc., coming into your bunk area to screw up this internal sleep clock.

In addition, and this is exciting, some studies indicate that melatonin, when taken as a supplement, can stop or slow down the spread cancer and make the immune system stronger. It can also slow down the aging process. That's right! These studies indicate that melatonin is able to reduce age-induced decline in the body's normal antioxidant system, and acts as a free radical scavenger and an anti-aging agent. 2

But, make sure your taking the right form of Melatonin. You want to take the synthetic form because it is safer to use because it is free from biological contaminants. The other form is made from ground up cow pineal gland, which can be contaminated with animal viruses.

I also want to share what I learned about the proper steps to helping your body get the rest it needs. First, don't drink any alcoholic beverages. They are usually prohibited by most companies anyway. Drinking alcoholic beverages, caffeinated beverages and energy drinks, are the worst drinks to have before bed. You tend to wake up a few hours later and have trouble falling back to sleep, leaving you groggy the next morning, which is really dangerous, making it difficult to focus on driving that next day.

Non-Alcoholic Beer

If you really like to have something that taste like beer at night, but does not have all the pitfalls of beer, try non-alcoholic beer.

Researchers in Spain (Daily Health News 10/11/12) evaluated subjects who drank non-alcoholic beer and found the subjects slept better. Not only did they fall asleep on average of 12 minutes faster, but they experienced 27% fewer movements while sleeping—meaningless tossing and turning. 3

Researchers believe that it's the bitter resins in hop compounds used in brewing for their aroma that do the trick. Hop compounds have sedative properties, soothing the central nervous system by raising levels of the neurotransmitter gamma-aminobutyric acid (GABA). This helps explain why non-alcoholic beer may help you not only get to sleep but sleep soundly and stay asleep. It has the hop compounds that make you drowsy, but not the alcohol that wakes you up later. 3

Technically speaking, non-alcoholic beers do have a tiny bit of alcohol in them, less than 0.5%. That does not meet the legal definition of an alcoholic beverage, which is any beverage with more than 0.5% of alcohol by volume.

Researchers found that it is best to drink a non-alcoholic beer roughly an hour before bed to get the most effect, and also noted that the hop compounds remain in your system all night. All non-alcoholic beers have approximately the same level of hop compounds. So it doesn't matter which brand you choose—any is likely to help you get to sleep. 3

Avoid non-alcoholic beer if:

1. You have trouble digesting gluten (a protein found in wheat, barley and rye), because most non-alcoholic (and alcoholic) beers contain gluten.
2. If you have type 1 or 2 diabetes and you're limiting carbs to keep your blood sugar in a healthy range. A non-alcoholic beer has roughly 13 grams of carbs.

If you have trouble falling asleep, here are some more recommendations:

1. Sublingual Melatonin—Melatonin, a hormone produced in the Pineal gland in the brain, helps to control sleep and wake cycles. Start with 1.5mg, 30 to 45 minutes before bedtime. If this doesn't help within three nights, try 3mg.

2. 5-Hydroxytrypophan (5-HTP)—The body uses this amino acid to manufacture the 'good mood' neurotransmitter, serotonin. It increases the body's serotonin production, promoting a sense of well-being and better resistance to stress. Start with 100mg one hour before bedtime. Increase to 200mg if the lower amount does not seem to do the trick.
3. Calcium and/or Magnesium—These supplements can help drivers who are deficient in these minerals (especially seniors) fall asleep by relaxing the nervous system. Try both to see which works best for you.

If you wake up and have trouble getting back to sleep, eat a light snack before bedtime. Some people wake up during the night because their blood sugar dips, triggering the adrenal glands to produce adrenaline.

CHAPTER 12

EATING ON THE ROAD

In order to save money, you need to plan your meals ahead of time. If you don't you could easily spend half you pay check eating at truck stops. You are driving a truck to make a living, so you need to discipline yourself to stick to the food you bring with you in the truck. Every once in awhile you will need a break from the routine, and will eat at the truck stop or some other restaurant that has easy access for your truck and trailer. But try to limit those restaurant meals to no more than once a week.

The type of meals I ate, and the food items I carried in my truck were pretty basic. You will need to decide how to best save money on meals that best suits your needs and tastes.

At the time I was driving, I was also a distributor for Herbalife. I brought their product called Herbalife 24, which is a powered protein based meal designed for athletes. I simply put two scoops in my 64 oz. water bottle, added some other healthy spices and that was my main meal. The Herbalife meal replacements saved me hundreds of dollars. They were good and satisfying. You can buy similar powder based meal replacement shakes, just shop around for the best price. You want one that can be mixed with water, not milk, unless you have a refrigerator in your truck that can store milk.

I also kept walnuts and almonds and various other nuts and fruits within easy reach in my center storage unit and dipped into these while driving. I also drank lots of water, V-8 juice, green tea, apple juice and various other drinks, all purchased at Costco. I would stock up on my favorite candy bar, Snickers. You simply cannot beat the 'per unit' cost of items at Costco. I did not have a refrigerator in the truck so I couldn't carry milk or any food that would spoiled quickly. That's why I recommend the meal replacement powders that can be mixed with water.

The point I want to make in this section is to make sure you take care of yourself. By eating well, exercising and getting enough rest you will help insure you can continue driving for as long as you want. The new stringent laws coming on line will make it impossible for unhealthy drivers to keep their commercial licenses.

While at Wal-Mart, in the Auto section, I purchased a center counsel storage box with cup holders, similar to what you would use between the seats of a pickup truck. I placed it right next to me in the truck and put all the stuff I would need for the road to keep me rolling with little or no stopping. I usually would drive a full 10 hours without stopping.

I kept all my drinks, power bars, couple apples, two or three juices, a snickers, my cell phone charger cord and other items in this center counsel. It was one of the best investments I made.

As a side note, drivers can no longer drive 10 or 11 hours straight. A new regulation that went into effect 7/1/2013, requires all commercial drivers to take a 30 minute break after being on duty 8 hours.

All of the health magazines and articles I have read that addressed the best way of eating; all agree that eating 5 to 6 small meals a day is the way to go. 1

I tried to do exactly that and found that these frequent meals helped me feel full and prevented me from making bad snack choices. I had all the right foods right next to me. My only vice was that one Snickers bar I would treat myself to around mid-day. So, eating in the truck is pretty easy and basic. If you do not stock up at Costco or Sams Clubs, you will end up spending way too much to stock your truck with all your favorite things to eat and drink.

Benefits of Apples

If you like apples, Costco sells these great green apples that are contained in a hard clear plastic case, which I found is perfect for the truck. If you break them out of the hard plastic case and put them in bags, the go bad very quickly. So keep them in the hard case and they will easily last 2 weeks. You should be eating at least 1 to 2 apples a day.

You know the old saying that an apple a day keeps the doctor away. Well there is actually some truth to that. Apples have high levels of nutritional content. Many of the vitamins and minerals in apples act together to provide you with more benefits than taking vitamins alone.2

Many of the known benefits of apples include the fact that the phytonutrients in apples can protect your brain from diseases like Alzheimer's and Parkinson's. These diseases have their roots from the breakdown of the brain.2

Also, apples have high levels of fiber which aides both digestive regularity and relief of constipation. Apples also help in the fight against many potentially fatal diseases, including some forms of cancer, heart disease, and type II diabetes. It can also help prevent problems such as hemorrhoids (truckers sit a lot) and Crohn's disease (www.Heart.org).2

Many of the apples benefits are found in the peel of the apple, so eat the whole apple, minus the stem and seeds. Researchers identified several compounds called Triterpenoids, in apple peel that has potent anti-growth properties against cancer cells in the liver, colon and breast. They also found that extracts from whole apples can reduce the number and size of mammary tumors in rats. 2

Apples have also been known to decrease the effects of asthma. They can also help in the fight against lung cancer and help reduce your risk of developing pancreatic cancer by up to 23%.2

In 2004, USDA scientists investigated over 100 foods to measure their antioxidant properties and found that two apples, Red Delicious and Granny Smith, ranked 12th and 13th respectively. That is an impressive fact. Eating a high fiber diet that apples provide, can reduce the risk of colorectal cancer. In addition, people who eat a diet rich in fruits, like apples, are 10 to 15% less likely to develop cataracts. You can't drive if your eyes are defective.2

So, I think I have made my case for carrying plenty of apples in your truck.

By the way, use the storage area under the lower bunk to store your extra water and drinks. If your truck is equipped with a heater located under the lower bunk, in the storage area, be careful not to stack stuff on top or right next to it. It creates a lot of heat when operating and will not run efficiently if the air flow is obstructed by boxes or other items.

You want to stay healthy out there on the road and I found that getting healthy was not about reaching a single goal and then thinking you have arrived! It is about realizing that those small daily choices make an impact on your whole life. Those small healthy choices add up, and over the weeks, months and years, they will help you maintain your health. With all the new rules for commercial drivers coming into effect and more changes on the horizon, if you allow yourself to become 'unhealthy', you may find yourself trying to renew you health card, and failing to pass the new stringent standards. No health card, no commercial driver's license. It will be suspended! It will be at that moment when you are going to wish you had made those tiny, daily healthy choices, which are in fact are just as easy to make as the unhealthy ones. They are just choices.

Benefits of Proper Teeth Cleaning and Flossing

Since we are on the topic of eating and staying healthy out there on the road, let me address brushing your teeth in the truck. I figured out a system that does not require being at any facility. I prepare a short glass of water, poured from one of the two 5 gallon containers I carry in the truck. After brushing my teeth with my electric toothbrush, I use an empty can to spit the toothpaste into, rinse my mouth out with water from in the glass I had previously prepared, and then spit the rinse water into the empty can. I then place that can into my plastic trash bag I have hanging off the arm rest of the passenger seat. I then rinse the toothbrush in the remaining clean water in the glass, dry it with a towel or air dry it. Then I throw the dirty water in the glass out the window, clean the glass and wipe it dry. I only mention this because you will not always have access to facilities that have running water, and sometimes the water at rest stops is not potable/ not drinkable and should therefore not be used to brush your teeth or rinse your toothbrush.

Brushing your teeth and flossing are critical to staying healthy out there on the road. There is a DIRECT relationship between brushing, flossing and regular 6 month visits to the dentist for teeth cleanings and your risk for heart disease, stroke and diabetic complications. The reason there is a direct link is that if you don't floss and have regular teeth cleanings you are at a higher risk for gum disease.

Gum disease is a bacterial infection which causes inflammation of the gums, in the presence of tarter trapped beneath the gums. This bacterial infection or gum disease can get into the blood stream and penetrate the walls of the small arteries of your heart. This triggers a reaction that causes the platelets to stick together; eventually growing so thick it begins to close off the artery and deprives the heart and brain of needed oxygen. This leads to a heart attack or stroke. 3

This oral bacterium is actually found in these clots and damaged tissues during autopsies after these poor people die. 3

So, regular brushing and flossing as well as regular teeth cleanings by your dentist helps prevent periodontal disease and gingivitis. Flossing removes bacteria and plaque, which can be absorbed into the blood stream. Then, as mentioned above, once it gets into the bloodstream, bad things start to happen.

I heard one dentist liken flossing your teeth to vacuuming in between the seats of your car after a two week road trip with a bunch of toddlers and young teens. It gets all those bits of food; French fries, cereal, whatever, and removes them before they can collect dust and start stinking the car up. I thought that was a pretty cool analogy. If you have ever done a deep cleaning under and between your car seats you know what I mean.

Benefits and Drawbacks of Coffee

Since we are on the topic of eating (and drinking) healthy, let me take this opportunity to address the consumption of coffee.

From what I saw on the road at truck stops, coffee is one of the leading items that are sold at truck stops. So I want to share the current information I have gleaned from various articles and scientific studies on the benefits and drawbacks of coffee. You can get the latest information about the benefits of coffee by simply typing in your internet search bar, 'Benefits of coffee'.

On the one hand coffee is loaded with free-radical fighting antioxidants, which helps explain its protective, anti-inflammatory effect against everything from type 2 diabetes to heart disease. Caffeine itself, which is a nervous system stimulant, leads to sharper focus and enhanced concentration. It can also improve your mood. But, get too much caffeine and the initial 'good feeling' can nosedive into restlessness, nervousness, insomnia and even muscle twitching. 4

Coffee is the single greatest source of antioxidants in the American diet. Ounce for ounce, other foods such as blueberries, pecans and cinnamon (all of which I recommend carrying in your truck) have more antioxidants than coffee, but are not as popular. 4

Coffee is loaded with polyphenols, which is a type of antioxidant found in many vegetables and berries. Polyphenols provide some very good health benefits. They destroy free radicals, which are rogue molecules that create inflammation. 4

One of the main compounds in coffee is xanthenes, which increases your metabolic rate, suppresses your appetite and enhances your physical and mental performance. 4

Many chronic illnesses, such as heart disease and type 2 diabetes are often caused or aggravated by inflammation. The more antioxidants in your diet, the less inflammation in your body. The cells in your body that can control intracellular inflammation processes are going to survive better under the stress of daily living. 4

Decaf coffee has just as many antioxidants as regular coffee, but the standard decaffeination process should worry any health conscious person. To take the caffeine from the bean, most coffee companies use chemical solvents, such as methylene chloride or ethyl acetate. The solvents are rinsed away at the end of the process, but there are concerns about chemical residue. But there is good news, there are companies selling coffee decaffeinated by a process called the Swiss Water Process, which uses water instead of chemicals. 4

Coffee has some unexpected benefits in that it may be helping to prevent type 2 diabetes. In one study by the Harvard School of Public Health, subjects who drank six or more cups of coffee a day lowered their risk of developing type 2 diabetes by 35 percent. Those who drank between four and six cups daily had a 28 percent risk reduction and other studies have shown a significant benefit with just one cup a day. So when all the evidence is weighed, the benefit is not restricted to those who drink the most. Caffeine is not the magic ingredient here, since decaf drinkers enjoy the same benefits in regards to preventing diabetes. Some researchers think a substance in coffee called chlorogenic acid slows the release of glucose into the bloodstream. Others think that it is coffee's antioxidants that help regulate the body's sensitivity to insulin. 4

There was also a study conducted in Finland and published in the Journal of the American Medical Association that also showed a link between drinking coffee and type 2 diabetes. They found that drinking three to four cups of coffee a day decreased risk of type 2 diabetes by 27 percent, and 10 cups a day lowered the risk by 55 percent. 4

Coffee contains antioxidants and minerals like magnesium that are beneficial for blood sugar metabolism and insulin sensitivity. 4

It should be noted that the studies showing the health benefits for type 2 diabetes are based on coffee that is black or with very little milk or sugar.

Coffee also confers some heart benefits. An Iowa Women's Health Study found that one to three cups of coffee lowered their risk of heart disease by 24 percent. Women who drank four to five cups a day were 33 percent less likely to die from any inflammatory disease. The beneficial ingredient is most likely the antioxidants. The foundation of heart disease is inflammation of the blood vessels, which is instigated and propagated by free radicals. Nothing combats free radicals like antioxidants. 4

For people with high cholesterol, there is a danger, because coffee contains two oily substances, cafestol and kahweol, that can raise blood levels of low density lipoprotein (LDL) which is the Bad cholesterol. The oils are released when coffee beans are brewed and easily pass through the metal filters used in French press and stovetop espresso pots. Paper filters, on the other hand, which are used in drip coffee machines, which are most often used at truck stops, trap the substances before they get to your cup, virtually eliminating any risk of an increase in cholesterol. 4

The caffeine in coffee could also safeguard your brain, in the case of depression, which millions of Americans suffer from. There is a Nurses' Health Study that shows rates of depression were lower when the subjects consumed coffee. The more coffee they consumed, the lower the levels of depression. Women who drank four or more cups of coffee a day experienced depression 20 percent less often. It appears from the study that caffeine is the ingredient that is adding this benefit, as those who drank decaf did not experience the same benefits as those who drank caffeinated coffee. 4

When caffeine enters the brain, it changes the levels of chemical messengers such as serotonin and dopamine, which are linked to feelings of joy and enthusiasm. Caffeine increases your energy levels and feelings of wellness, two things that can have an impact on depression. 4

If all the above were not enough to make coffee look good, some studies also show a 30 percent reduced risk of developing Parkinson's disease among coffee drinkers, for similar reasons. That's because Parkinson's is caused by the loss of brain cells that make dopamine, a chemical instrumental in movement and fine motor control. 4

There are at least six other studies that indicated that people who drink coffee on a regular basis are up to 80 percent less likely to develop Parkinson's. In fact the newest Parkinson's drugs contain a derivative of caffeine. 4

Coffee also has a protective effect against colon cancer. A recent study from the European Journal of Cancer Prevention showed that colon cancer was 24 percent lower among those who drank 4 or more cups of coffee per day, than those who seldom drink coffee. 4

Scientists speculate that anti-mutagenic components in coffee and caffeine inhibit the cancer causing effect of various micro-organisms. 4

Researchers from Harvard University found that those drinking one cup a day had a 13 percent risk reduction of gallstone disease. Those drinking 2 to 3 cups of coffee a day had a 21 percent risk reduction, and those who drank 4 or more cups a day had a 33 percent risk reduction of gallstone disease. 4

If all the above were not amazing enough, it also turns out that the caffeine and other chemicals in coffee help moderate asthma attacks. The caffeine acts as a natural bronchodialater. The chemical theophyline exists naturally in coffee. For years theophyline was the primary pharmaceutical weapon against asthma. 3 or more cups of coffee a day can help relieve the symptoms of asthma. 4

And finally, another recent study published in the Journal of Alzheimer's Disease stated that drinking 5 cups of coffee a day could lower your chances of Alzheimer's. As little as 3 cups of coffee a day cuts your risk of mental decline by over 50 percent. 4

I was not a coffee drinker before starting my truck driving experience, but after finding this information I have now begun to drink coffee more often.

As you have read, there are several benefits to drinking coffee, but I am sure you have heard the old saying about <u>too</u> much of a good thing.

Caffeine, like nicotine and amphetamines, can be highly addictive. Regularly drinking about 6 ounces of drip coffee is enough to create a physical dependence. It acts on the motivational brain mechanisms that make you want to use more, regardless of how it makes you feel.

Overindulging in caffeine can make you feel crummy. That's because excess caffeine sparks the adrenal glands into releasing stress hormones, like adrenaline and cortisol that can put the brain and body into a panic like state. This is unpleasant and unhealthy. The more caffeine you have in your system the more often you trigger the body's emergency response system. If you keep setting off this internal siren every 10 minutes, you will burn out. 4

Caffeine's artificial energy boost can also distance people from their natural energy rhythms. Caffeine's false energy effect can encourage people to overdo and discourage people from taking recovery breaks when they should. Pretty soon you are both wired and tired. 4

Over time, the adrenal glands may not make enough cortisol to maintain a baseline of energy, a condition referred to as adrenal fatigue. You are pushing an organ that doesn't have the reserves to respond to the stimulant anymore. 4

In athletes caffeine is one of the few legal drugs scientifically proven to boost performance. It mobilizes fat stores, freeing up energy for hard working muscles. It also draws more calcium into muscles, thereby strengthening their contraction. And it triggers the brain to release endorphins, which raises the person's pain threshold. 4

The key to receiving all of the benefits of coffee is to drink it in moderation, around 3 to 4 cups a day. Don't drink coffee too close to bedtime and keep the 'extras' like sugar and cream to a bare minimum. Try to buy organic coffee's that are pesticide free. You simply don't want those poisons in your system. Coffee's healing properties are strongest when it is freshly brewed.

Some alternatives to coffee include an herb called guarana. The active compound in guarana is guaraine, which is a member of the caffeine family. I was introduced to guarana about 2 years ago to help me focus. Unlike regular caffeine, guarana is full of healthy fatty acids. These good fatty acids give guarana a slow release. Coffee overheats and excites the body, but guarana has a cooling action that revitalizes and relaxes your body. 4

Key Aspects of Coffee

Below is a little guide on four key aspects of coffee to edify you and help you make a decision on which type of coffee might be best for you.

The Bean: The two most commonly used coffee plant varieties are *Arabica* and *Robusta*. Arabica beans are considered to be more flavorful, therefore more expensive and usually found in gourmet coffees. The less expensive Robusta beans are used primarily to make instant coffee and have about twice the caffeine as Arabica. 4

Roast: Darker roasts, like French Roasted coffee beans, contain less caffeine than lighter roasts because some of the caffeine burns off during the roasting process. Roasting also degrades the polyphenol antioxidants. So if you are looking for a bigger kick, choose a lighter roast. 4

Grinds: Generally the finer the grind, the more caffeine you will extract. Whether you want a fine or coarse grind, depends on how long the water will be in contact with the beans. If it's just a few seconds, like espresso, a finer grind maximizes contact between the water and the surface area of the beans. If it's a few minutes like a French press, a coarser grind ensures a smooth, mellow cup of coffee. Espresso packs less caffeine per serving than drip coffee, but espresso will give you a quicker buzz if you drink it in one or two gulps. 4

Aroma: I absolutely love the smell of coffee beans roasting, and coffee brewing. In one study, just the smell of coffee was enough to increase people's typing speed. Roasted coffee beans contain roughly 800 aromatic compounds. Coffee's aromatic compounds, and flavor, are influenced by geography. Elevation, moisture and temperature are just three examples of what makes coffee grown in Central America taste different from coffee grown in East Africa. 4

Drinking coffee fresh helps maximize flavor and prevents oxidation. Old stale coffee should be avoided.

Drink your coffee black, or at least keep the cream and sugar to a bare minimum. These add-ons diminish the rewards and add calories.

Don't drink coffee close to bed time, because your brain and your body both require rest. And be aware of those energy shots, they contain *synthetic* caffeine.

Benefits of Raw Unfiltered Honey

Now that I have covered coffee, I now want to convince you to avoid sugars and artificial sweeteners that you may put into that coffee. Raw sugar is simply bad for you. Some people refer to sugar as a poison. I am not going to go into all the dangers and draw backs of sugar, because they have been fairly publicized in the media. I instead would like you to consider using raw unfiltered honey. Some people cannot handle raw unfiltered. So do some research above and beyond what I offer here to determine if raw unfiltered honey is a good alternative to sugar for you.

Raw honey is concentrated nectar that comes from flowers. The ingredients in raw honey are similar to the ones found in fruits. Raw unfiltered honey contains the actual bee pollen. Bee Pollen is a top 10 super food for its nutritional benefits, protein and active enzyme levels. 5

Honey bees collect a substance called Propolis, a resin for building their bee hives. They use it to seal and sterilize the hive from outside contamination. Propolis has been used since the time of Hippocrates to heal external wounds and internal conditions. It is a natural antibiotic and antiseptic. It has been proven to exhibit antioxidant effects with antimicrobial and anti-inflammatory properties. It is known to be helpful in boosting the immune system and supporting liver health. 5

Unprocessed natural honey benefits the body as one of the richest sources of amylase. This is an essential enzyme that helps break down starches into sugars. 5

Raw unfiltered honey is a great alternative sweetener because it enters the blood stream slowly and maintains a balanced flow of energy, instead of the standard highs and lows of sugar or refined honey. 5

So, do a little research on your own to determine is raw unfiltered honey is right for you.

CHAPTER 13

VEHICLE INSPECTIONS

Lyrics from Country Song, 'Highway Patrol', by Junior Brown

I got a star on my car and one on my chest,
A gun on my hip and the right to arrest,
I'm the guy who's the boss on this highway,
So watch out what you're doing when you're driving my way,
If you break the law, you'll hear from me I know,
I'm working for the state,
I'm the 'Highway Patrol'.

If you end up working for a large established company like Schneider National, their reputation for safety and following the DOT rules goes a long way in helping you stay on the road, and by pass weight stations. Let me explain.

On the windshield of your truck will be a blue or green plastic transponder. As you approach a weight station, you will see notices on the highway advising all commercial vehicles to pull into the weigh station. You <u>may</u> then see notices on the highway advising commercial

drivers, "PREPASS Follow In Cab Signals" which is instructing you to follow the commands given on your transponder.

There are three lights on your transponder. Green means you can keep going and do not need to stop. Red means you must pull into the weight station, and follow the directions given on the signs.

About a half mile from the weight station you will pass under a device that looks like a large light post with long 'radar' looking devices attached to it.

This reads your transponder and gives the weight station information about your truck. You may also pass over two rubber strips in the road which gives the weight station a preliminary reading on your weight.

If you have a poor record of driving overweight, you will always get pulled in. But if you have a clean record, most of the time you will get the green light, allowing you to stay on the freeway and bypass the weight station. If you receive a red light, you must pull in and follow the signs. Usually these signs will advise you to slow down to 5 or 10 mph as you drive over the scales. If you weight is within limits, you will be advised to continue. If there is a weight problem, or the inspector spots something on the truck he wants to inspect, the sign or light ahead of you will flash red and you will have to pull the truck forward and park in the designated parking area. You then have to bring in all your paperwork, which is usually all located in one binder, kept in the door, as well as your Bill of Lading for the load you are carrying.

Hazardous Materials and Placards

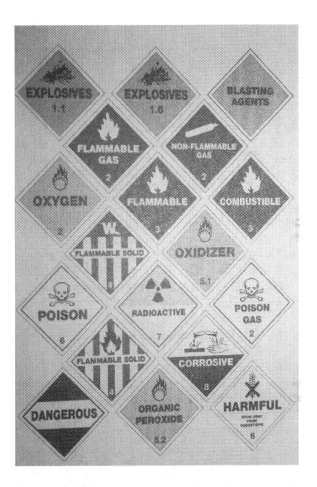

If you are carrying any Hazardous Material that requires you to place placards on your trailer, you are <u>required</u> to stop at ALL weight stations, regardless of a green light on your transponder.

Here is some advice that was passed on to me by a Kansas State trooper at a weight station. If your Hazardous Material placards are made from just stiff paper or adhesive back material, you should place additional material in the placard holder to prevent the placard from being sucked out by the wind.

On one of my first Hazardous Material loads I was going through a weight station and was advised via load speaker that my trailer did not have all the necessary placards, and was told to park my truck and bring in all my paperwork.

I started to panic. I know these fines can be really steep, and if the violation cannot be fixed, I will receive an 'Out of Service' order which means I am grounded until it is fixed. The inspector pointed out the nose of the trailer (just behind the cab of the truck) did not have the required placard. I was at a loss as to how the placard was removed since I just put it there earlier in the day and I had not stopped.

The inspector (Kansas State Trooper) advised me that the area behind the cab, in front of the nose of the trailer is subject to a vacuum type conditions created as you drive. The wind/ vacuum conditions sucked the stiff paper placard right out of the holder, because the holder had gaps that were too large.

The inspector showed me a trick that would guarantee the placard would stay in place. You take a standard wire hanger, cut the hanger and make a 'W' out of the wire. Then place the wire inside the plastic holder, on top of the placard. This closes off the large gaps and prevents the placard from being sucked out of the nose of the trailer. The officer did not cite me, because I was prepared with an extra placard. He just completed an inspection report.

By the way, when you are doing your own Pre-Trip, Post-Trip and TIV inspections, ensure that the truck engine is off. It is really unsafe for you to be under your truck or trailer with the engine running. I remember one of the few times our instructors actually yelled at us was when a student started to crawl under the trailer to check if the fifth wheel was securely locked across the king pin, or trying to get a closer look at the brake drums, while the truck engine was running.

CHAPTER 14

VEHICLE SPEED

Lyrics From the Country Song: 'Nitro Express' by Bill Kirchen

Well I was pulling up a grade known as the Devil's Crest;
All 36 tons on a run called The Nitro Expresss;
There was nothing but curves running from the top on down;
And at the bottom of the grade sat a quiet little country town;
I was drivin' off the top when she jarred and the drive shaft broke;
I started pumping the brakes, watching em'go in a big cloud of smoke;
To keep her upright I had to do my best;
I guess the runaway bomb known as the Nitro Express;
There were 36 tons of dead neck Steele, over 18 tires and spokeless wheels;
I had to ride her down and I couldn't just freeze or there would be a big hole
Where the little town used to be;
That old trailer started lean'in every time that I took another curve;
My hands started sweat'in, man I knew I was losing my nerve;
I was cussing every rock and every inch of that Devil's Crest;
Fighting with the wheel of a rig called the Nitro Express;
I'd side swipe the mountain, thought I'd slow her down by her side;

When those sparks started flying, man it looked like the
4th of July;
I finally got her stopped, but mister I'm a going to confess;
That's the last run I'm taking on a rig called the Nitro
Experss.

When you first start driving an 18 wheeler, there is usually no problem with driving too fast. You are naturally being very cautious. Everything is relatively new and your skills are just not as developed as they need to be. You recognize this and keep your speed down.

But as you progress, you become more familiar with the truck, more confident in your abilities and are inclined to begin driving faster than you should. This is especially true when driving down hill.

I learned very quickly, why you are taught at your driving school or during company orientation as well as during the on the road training, to downshift to a lower gear BEFORE you start your downhill decent.

On my first big downhill grade I thought I had more time to downshift, and as the truck began to pick up speed, I tried to downshift, only to find I was unable to get the truck in a lower gear. The pressure that the weight of the truck was placing on the transmission was preventing me from down shifting. The truck continued to pick up speed and I began to panic, because now, not only was I coasting out of control, I was unable to get the truck into any gear. I immediately realized I was in serious trouble. I quickly applied the brakes in a stabbing fashion, until the truck slowed to about 10 mph, then quickly shifted into a lower gear, where it should have been in the first place.

My message here is to be very cautious with downhill grades. As you gain more experience and travel the same routes you will have a better idea of what gear you should be in. I saw dozens of trucks pulled off the side of the road with smoking brakes. They simply were in a gear that was too high for the grade, going too fast down the hill and their brakes heated up. Each of them is lucky their brakes didn't fail and result in a crash.

There is also a rule of thumb that whatever gear you were in coming up the hill, use the next lower gear to go down the other side. In the meantime strictly follow the recommendations in your manual you should get when you attend your company orientation.

Again, in relation to the violations listed near the end of this book, when I added up all the speeding related citations/violations for commercial vehicles in the U.S. alone for 2012, there were 128,888 violations reported. That is a lot of violations for speeding. So, slow down.

The state and local law enforcement agencies are out there and actively citing truckers who speed.

In addition, there were 2,949 citations issued in 2012 for possession of a Radar Detector in commercial vehicles. Just in case you were unclear about radar detectors, they are illegal, and law enforcement officials have ways to detect those devices. They also will cite if they simply see one in your truck while they are conducting a roadside inspection. Just drive responsibly and you won't need to worry about trying to avoid a speeding ticket. It's that simple!

CHAPTER 15

WORKING WITH YOUR DISPATCHER

This may be one the most important topics to help keep your stress level down as you muddle through your first few months. Your dispatcher, also known as a DBL (Driver Business Leader), is the person who assigns you loads and works with you to help you become a successful driver.

In the beginning you should use your dispatcher anytime you have questions or problems. He is there to answer your questions and be there for anything you may need. It is to the dispatcher's advantage to bring you along and assist you every way he can. The better prepared you are, the less work he has to do. He is investing his time to make you more comfortable and competent.

You should treat your dispatcher like he has complete control over your career. Treat him with ultimate respect. Even when things go bad or not as planned, DO NOT take it out on your dispatcher. If you piss off your dispatcher, he/she can make life hell for you. They have no control over the most situations. It is not their fault that some things go wrong. Remember, it is to their advantage that things go smoothly, because it means less work for them.

Once you become more proficient and experienced, you will not be calling or relying on your dispatcher as much.

When I started, I was <u>very</u> lucky in being assigned one of the best dispatchers in the company, Greg Russell. In looking back, Greg probably the only reason I stayed as long as I did. There were many times when I simply could not understand my assignment. Instead of being written in plain English, pre-assignments are written in some in-house code that often made no sense. It was very frustrating trying to decipher what the assignment was directing me to do. Greg was always there to explain what was involved in the assignment and admitted that at times even he did not completely understand the assignment. Whether that was true or not, it made me feel better. It took me a good 4 months before I became comfortable with deciphering the pre-assignments correctly.

While I was on the road I would meet other new drivers who were so depressed because their dispatchers treated them like crap. Of course I didn't know the whole story. They may have brought it upon themselves by being abusive to their dispatcher. All I know is, it is in your best interest to be very civil, and respectful of your dispatcher <u>at all times.</u> That does not mean you can't share some job related issues with him. He needs to know how you're doing and what job related issues you are having problems with. Just remember, he has no control over the company or how they do business.

Suggestions to Help You Get Home on Time

If you are having personal issues that will require you to go home as soon as possible, you should obviously share that with your dispatcher, so he can start finding you loads to get you closer to home.

Sometimes getting you home is not as easy as you might think. In case you didn't know, you are at the bottom of the food chain. As a new driver you get the loads that all the other senior or independent drivers don't want. Most independent drivers are part of a system where they pick their own loads, sometimes weeks in advance. So you get stuck with the 'low value loads' like paper rolls, recycled cardboard, wood pallets, salt. So be patient with your dispatcher.

Remember to send your dispatcher <u>respectful</u> messages every day, reminding them of your need to get home. Also communicate with your dispatcher if you have to get home for a doctor appointment. If your doctor appointment is on a Friday, I advise telling them it is on Wednesday. Don't count on getting home on the day you need to. On two occasions I needed to get home on a specific date, by a specific time. Well, my dispatcher did his best, but I did not arrive until 6 hours after my appointments. So, I had to re-schedule my appointments.

If you are planning some time off, plan your doctor appointments near the end of that time off period. Because, again, getting you home on the day you want to be home is not an exact science. It all depends on what loads are available. Sometimes they have to send you in the opposite direction in order to find you the best opportunity to get a load back home. You may have to pull 2 or 3 loads before they can find a load for you to get home. Be patient and plan ahead.

CHAPTER 16

ORGANIZING THE INTERIOR
OF YOUR TRUCK

Organizing the interior of your truck, so you can reach most of the things you will need while you are driving, can vastly improve your efficiency and increase the miles you are able to log in each day. Remember the more miles you drive each day, the more money you make.

Use Voice Recorder on Cell Phone

As you begin to drive make a note of the occasions where you are forced to pull off the highway to get something in the truck that was located in an area of truck that was not accessible while you were driving. Instead of making mental notes, I would use my cell phone program called 'Voice Recorder'. This program should be put right on your start up screen. Anytime I wanted to remember something, I simply grabbed my cell phone, which was always within easy reach. While keeping my eyes of the road, I pushed the Voice Recorder icon, and recorded my thoughts, then stopped recording. It saves trying to find a piece of paper while you're driving (not safe) and writing a note to yourself while driving (again, not safe). Continue this process and it will help you organize your truck so you have the things you need most often within reach.

I would also use this voice recorder if I needed to record something quickly, like the license plate number and vehicle description of a reckless or drunk driver to relay to the information to State Patrol. If I witnessed an accident or saw someone broke down, I would use the voice recorder to quickly record whatever facts I needed to remember, including the mile marker, for later use as appropriate.

3 in 1 Power Port

When I started driving, I found I simply did not have enough power ports or charging stations within easy reach as I was driving. I only had one power port/plug on the dash. To fix that, I found this 3 in 1 power station at a truck stop that plugs into any power plug and immediately turns it in 3 power ports. Now I had power ports for my cell phone, and two other items that I would occasionally need while driving.

I know this is a random item, but I just remembered it, so I will mention it in here. I highly recommend an electric toothbrush. They do a much better job of cleaning your teeth. There are plenty of charging stations in most of these new trucks, so you should have no problem finding one that you can dedicate just for your electric toothbrush.

Another random item, keep your shaving kit in a handy and permanent location. When I first started I would put my shaving kit in a different bag or compartment every day and then spend way too much time trying to remember where I put it. So find a permanent location for it since you use it every day.

Artificial Turf for Truck Steps

While working in a truck, you are constantly battling to keep the inside of your truck clean. It takes no time at all before your truck floor is covered with little rocks, mud and dirt. I keep a small hand broom in the cab and often sweep it out. Some drivers hook up an air hose via the air system that powers your truck seas. They just blow out the truck every day.

An old trucker showed me a really handy item for the outside of the truck that goes a long way in helping keep all that dirt and mud out of your truck. The side of my truck had two steps leading up to the cab. Those steps are steel and have holes in them the size of a dime. Go to Home Depot and buy a piece of astro turf or a fake grass matt that has a ridged backing. Cut two pieces that fit both your steel steps leading up to your cab. Then secure them to the steps with plastic ties that have been fed through the holes in your steel steps. Use as many plastic ties as you feel you need. I would recommend installing a tie down every 6 inches. Now you have a mat you can clean your boots off with before you enter the cab. Pretty cool right?

Make it a rule that you never go into your bunk area with your boots on. That will help keep the dirt from being tracked into that area.

I also kept a real soft and comfortable bath mat on the floor right next to my bed. When I get up in my bare feet, it is a lot nicer to step onto that then the cold floor. In addition it can be easily thrown into the washer when needed.

Another item that I wish I had discovered earlier has to do with the sun visors in my truck. In the hot summer months I often had to drive with the sun shining on the side of my face because the sun visor did not go back far enough to block the sun. Just by accident, during the fall, I discovered that the sun visors can be adjusted along the entire length of the steel rod they are attached to. When I discovered this I felt so stupid. All this time all I had to do was pull on the visor when it was down to adjust it. I wish they would design car visors the same way.

Seat Organizers

Another tool that I found to very helpful are those organizers you slip over the back of your seat. They have numerous pockets for maps and various other items. I had one for both the driver and passenger seats. In that organizer I would place things on the side pocket like a magnifying glass that I would use when I looked at my maps. I found it a lot easier to do my trip planning and map reading with the map opened up over the steering wheel. This is done when the truck is stopped of course. I could simply reach over my right shoulder grab my magnifying glass, which had a built in light (recommended) to read my maps. Then simply replace it in the same side pocket I got it from, without even looking.

Work Gloves

One of the most important items you will need every day will be gloves that you use strictly of fueling your truck. Diesel is messy as well the new DEF (Diesel Exhaust Fluid) required on new trucks. I recommend buying those gloves designed for handling fuels and chemicals. Keep those gloves right in the side pocket of the driver's door. When you stop at a truck stop, copy down your mileage, and then get out of the truck to begin the process of paying for your fuel with your company fuel card.

Fueling

At the fuel pump input all your information, driver number, mileage, truck number, some states requires license plate number. Then after getting approval, reach inside your driver door side pocket and grab your fueling gloves. Remember, the truck has two tanks, one on each side, as well as the separate tank for the DEF. After starting the fuel on the driver's side, start filling the tank on the passenger side of the truck. Remember, DO NOT remove and hang up the pump on the driver's side first, because then the pump on the passenger side will stop as well.

Be sure as you are inserting the nozzle into the tanks, that they are securely fastened, or they may fall out, and pour diesel all over the fuel island. As your truck is fueling, take this time to wash your windshield and mirrors.

As soon as you finish fueling take your gloves off and immediately put them back inside the driver door side pocket. Do not climb up into the truck and get fuel residue from your gloves all over the seat, steering wheel and gear shift.

As I drove more hours each day, I found the heels of my hands were sore. So I went to Home Depot and purchased a pair of padded driving gloves. They had padding everywhere the hand made contact with the wheel. My hands felt a lot better. I only used these gloves for driving. As soon as I stopped the truck, I took the gloves off and threw them up on the dash board. I did not put them on again until I was ready to drive. This helped me keep them clean and free of grease and diesel fuel.

CHAPTER 17

ON THE ROAD

Lyrics from Country Song, 'On the Road Again', by Willie Nelson

On the road again,
I can't wait to get on the road again,
Goin' places that I've never been,
Seein' things that I may never see again,
And I can't wait to get on the road again.

10 Second Lane Change

One of the first things you learn, or at least I did, was how to do a 10 second lane change. I know it sounds simple and you might be thinking, come on, and get on with the good stuff; I don't need to hear about this elementary crap.

Well, this elementary crap saved my bacon a few times. The principle is simple. Any time you change lanes, first signal and of course check <u>ALL</u> your mirrors to make sure it's clear. Then <u>slowly</u> begin your lane change as you count to 10. By the time you reach 10, you should have completed your lane change. That is how slow and deliberate your lane changes should be. There were a few times early in my driving, that I simply did not see the <u>really small</u> car next to me. If I had not taken my time, I would have had a preventable accident on my record and perhaps caused a severe accident. Luckily the 'small' car honked their horn and I returned to my original lane, very embarrassed and angry at myself for getting that close to an accident. I see other truckers make fast lane changes all the time, but all I can say is that some day it is going to bit them in the butt big time. There are plenty of accident reports where the truck caused accidents with injuries and deaths due to the driver making severe lane changes, often without even signaling. So, a word of advice, take your time on your lane changes.

In relation to the statistics on violations by truckers listed near the end of this book, truckers were cited 9,079 for improper lane changes in 2012 alone. So, take your time, and do slow lane changes.

IPods, E-books, Sirius Radio

While driving, you will find that most states have some pretty long stretches. You will simply set your cruise control and enjoy the scenery. If you own an apple i-pod or some similar device that you can download audible e-books on, this can really help the trip go by faster. There are a few web sites which allow you to download their e-books free. Other sites charge a minimal fee. You would be surprised at the number of books you can go through in any given month, and how quickly you can increase your knowledge on a variety of topics, depending on the books you listen to. This is also a great opportunity to learn that 2nd language you never had time for. You literally have hundreds of free hours available to you. There is no excuse. I used to love listening to the military spy & murder type books, some fiction, some non-fiction.

Of course while you are listening to these e-books, you need to be paying attention to your driving and remain aware of any problems the truck may develop. This includes continuing to check you gauges, scanning traffic ahead of you, and checking your mirrors for problems with the trailer, vehicles approaching from behind, etc.

You may also want to look into Sirius Satellite Radio. It really is a must. When using your regular truck radio, it never fails that by the time you find a good radio station you are quickly out of range and searching for another one. Sirus is so convient and it has every type of music and programming you could possible want. If you are not adept at installing one, have a friend help you. If you are friends with one of the company mechanics, he could help you as well.

In the case of bad rain or snow storms, you should be 100% focused on the driving and not be distracted by any radio or e-books. You will need to be completely focused on the road in order to stay out of trouble. Winter driving is stressful! It requires all of your attention and you get tired quickly. I go into more information on winter driving later in the book.

King Pin Locks

If the company you work for requires the use of a king pin lock, make sure you practice putting it on and taking it off. Study how the lock operates as you turn the key. It will make it a lot easier once you have to do it for real in less than ideal circumstances. They are a little tricky to get onto the king pin unless you have practiced it and are familiar with the operation of the key and how it operates the locking mechanism.

The only situations that I personally used the king pin lock were when I was going to be away from my truck and trailer for any extended period of time. Let me walk you through a typical situation.

Alternate Parking Locations

As I gained experience and was assigned longer distance loads, I became more familiar with the major highways and routes I would take in the various states, I began to note where there were good places to park my rig that were near good restaurants and movie theaters. I love going to the movies. So I would begin to use my laptop computer to search for large movie complexes that were near the end of my 11 hour driving limit set by the Department of Transportation. Remember, you have 14 hours from the time you begin your day to get 11 hours of driving time in. The remaining three hours are used for fueling, scaling your load, meals, breaks, pre-trip and post-trip inspections. Those extra 3 hours can get used up in a hurry if you are not paying attention.

Normally, I will re-fuel as soon as I drop my load, and while waiting for my next load. When I get my next load, I will have already fueled up and am prepared to just drive. Using your down time wisely will soon become second nature as you gain experience. I often will drive a straight 10 to 11 hours with few stops. At the end of my day, I will again re-fuel, there-by being prepared to just hit the road as soon as I wake up after my mandatory 10 hour break.

Before logging on for the day, I would have scoped out possible places to park after driving for 9 or 10 hours. This step was a very important part of my pre-trip planning. Specifically, I would look for large movie theater complexes. Next to or adjacent to the movie theaters, I will usually find large shopping centers, including stores such as Home Depot, Lowes, Costco or Wal-Mart. Any large shopping center will have lots of open space for parking over night. You will also want to take this pre-planning step.

Later, as you actually approach your potential parking spot for the night, keep your eyes open for the location of your favorite restaurants and the actual location of the movie theaters.

Be VERY careful as you maneuver your truck and trailer. Do Not get trapped into a situation you cannot get out of. Most driveways and access points to large centers <u>are not</u> designed for your truck and trailer. Shopping centers have specific routes for trucks. Most entrances are designed only for cars, and if you try to go in through these car routes, you will get your truck and trailer jammed into a situation where you may run over landscaping and sprinkler heads with your trailer wheels due to the tight turns. This is a mistake made by new drivers all the time due to lack of experience and failure to realize just how limited you are in regards to where you can maneuver that fifty-three foot trailer.

Trailer/Load Security

Find a spot that is as far away from the main buildings as possible. Then find a permanent fixture of some type to back your trailer up against. I would usually find a light post, which was encased in concrete three feet high, designed to prevent cars from knocking them down accidently. I would back my trailer up to within two inches of this post. You will need to get out a few times to insure you don't actually hit the post and cause damage. You want to have that post right up against the trailer door that has to open first. This gives you a little added security to prevent your load from being stolen while you are away.

Even if thieves were successful in cutting your lock off, they would not be able to get your trailer door open to access your load. They would have to knock down the fifty foot lamp post. I think you get the point here. You can use any permanent object to block those trailer doors from opening.

Note: If you are carrying any hazardous material and your trailer has placards posted, you are not allowed to leave your truck for extended periods. So, in that case you are out of luck as far as going to the movies. With hazardous material loads it is best to just stay with your standard truck stops and rest stops.

After you have parked in such a manner as to mitigate the chances of someone cutting your lock off and opening your trailer doors to steal your cargo, move to the next step. Now, you need to drop your trailer and pull your truck forward about 10 feet. Get your king pin lock out and put a small plastic bag over the opening of the lock. This plastic bag is to keep grease from the king pin off your lock.

Now, crawl under the trailer and push the king pin lock onto the king pin. Then push the lock in and turn the key to lock it in place. Remember you should have practiced this several time already, otherwise you are going to get frustrated when things don't seem to work right.

Once the king pin is in place, back your truck up under the nose of the trailer, but DO NOT hit the king pin. The purpose of the king pin is to prevent anyone from hooking up to your trailer and stealing it.

Now you are ready to lock up your truck and go eat and enjoy a movie. Before you lock your truck up, be sure to pull the curtains over your windshield and side windows so no one can see inside. Someone snooping around will not know if you are in the truck or not.

So now you have four levels of security. You have your war lock on the trailer door, in addition to any seals the shipper put on. You have your trailer backed into a solid object to prevent the doors from opening. You have a king pin lock on to prevent someone from just backing into your trailer and stealing it. In addition, you have your truck backed in under the nose of the trailer. If someone were to break into your truck and somehow able to move your truck, they still would not be able to hook into your trailer due to the king pin lock.

Again, remember to use one of those small plastic shopping bags to help keep grease from the king pin from getting on the king pin lock. Just place the plastic bag over the hole of the king pin lock as you push the lock up onto the king pin.

These steps are just part of your job. I know it seems a little excessive, but it really isn't. It is your job to secure your load before you leave it for any extended period. I would do this anytime I was away from the truck for more than one hour. That took place when I would go to the movies and eat out. But there was an occasion when I was in New Orleans and had a delivery scheduled for the next morning. Even though I was parked at a truck stop, which is fairly secure, I went through all these steps before I rented a car and did the tourist thing down Bourbon Street.

Bourbon Street/ French Quarter

I was not impressed with the whole French Quarter/ Bourbon Street scene. I found it incredibly dirty and somewhat dangerous. Locals would warn me not to go down this street or that street after dark, and remark about people who have been robbed or murdered down those streets after dark.

I am still glad I visited the French Quarter/ Bourbon Street area. Now I know what it's about, and I have no desire to return. But it was a worthwhile experience. I saw it as a place where young people go to get drunk and get in trouble. I guess I am just too old for that stuff now. It just does not appeal to me. When I was a teen or in my 20's, yes, this would be a cool place to go, like when New Orleans was in the Super Bowl. But I am just an old conservative guy now and lean more towards places I don't have to keep on high alert for muggers.

Another neat trick I discovered on the road to clean your glasses or sunglasses. I discovered a technique to give you clean and streak free lenses. When I am at a truck stop or rest stop, I clean the lenses on my glasses with the liquid hand soap. Then rinse it well. Then instead of drying them with paper towels, which always leave some streaks, I hold my glasses under the hot air hand dryers which will dry my glasses completely streak free in only 30 seconds.

Before I end this chapter, I want to address getting lost.

> Lyrics from Country Song: Give Me Forty Acres", by Red
> Simpson

> Give me forty acres and I'll turn this rig around;
> It's the easiest way that I found;
> Some guys can turn on a dime or turn it right downtown;
> But I need forty acres to turn this rig around

Even with highly accurate maps and state-of-the-art navigation systems, you will occasionally get lost. Getting lost, making a wrong turn, driving by your destination and then trying to find somewhere to safely turn your truck and trailer around, all can be very frustrating and stressful.

On one occasion my on board navigation system sent me down a narrow street that just did not look right. So I stopped the truck, got out and walked ahead about 300 feet and found that there was no way my truck and trailer would make the turn ahead. I would have ended up hitting a fire hydrant and tearing up someone's lawn. So I got back into my truck and slowly began to back down the street. As I approached the intersection, I stopped the truck, got out and flagged down a policeman. I told him what happened and he was happy to stop traffic for me so I could back all the way through the intersection and get back on the right road.

When you drive long haul, you will be driving all over the country and will rarely go to the same shipper or receiver twice. You will often get lost because directions given by your on board navigation system will sometimes be wrong. It is very frustrating but no navigation system is 100% reliable. Several times I had to ignore what my company navigation system was telling me and I had to rely on my own commercial trucking navigation system (Garmin). I have also had to simply pull over and call the location and ask them for directions.

When you have line hauls or dedicated runs, you will know the route in no time at all, and you won't need your map or navigations systems anymore, unless you're trying to get around a freeway closure.

In another situation in Chicago, my on board navigation sent me down what looked like a residential street. Sure enough it was and I got jammed in situation where I could not move the truck. I had to remember every trick I knew to maneuver the truck and trailer out before I could start backing out of that residential street. I called Chicago PD and advised them I needed a unit to stop traffic for me, but after 2 hours, they never showed up. A local resident offered to help me, and I told him I had already called Chicago PD for assistance. He started to laugh and said they are far too busy to respond to something like this. He said they will never show up. He then left. So I stood there, with the back of my trailer ready to back into the intersection, but I couldn't because I had no one to guide me and watch my trailer as I backed into the intersection. I simply could not do it safely without help. In addition, when the light turned green, it was only green for 15 seconds. That is not nearly enough time to safely back a truck and trailer through an intersection. So, there I was stuck, blocking residents from entering the street, with no way to move the rig.

Then I noticed about 8 teens loitering on the corner that appeared to be gang members. So I approached them and said to them, "Hey, you want to do something fun?" I then told them I needed them to stop traffic in all directions and guide my trailer though the intersection. Of course they wanted to know how much I was going to pay them, to which I said nothing. But they agreed anyway, and did a great job of keeping traffic stopped so I could safely get the truck backed through the intersection and back on my way.

I know, that may have been ill advised, but I was thinking outside the box and saw an opportunity to get out of a bad situation sooner rather than <u>much, much</u> later.

I know it is easy to say, but when you get yourself into a situation where you are lost, make a wrong turn or simply can't locate your destination, <u>don't go into panic mode</u>!

I remember dozens of times where I drove by my destination, and had to fight the over whelming urge to just whip a U-turn. I knew 'technically' I could have done it lots of times; I had the room and no traffic, but it simply is not safe to do in a tractor and trailer and it was against company policy. I have heard stories of drivers who simply did not see the trailer that was making the u-turn and ran right under the trailer. Then there are the pictures I have seen of trailers stuck in ditches where the driver poorly judged the U-turn and ended up putting the trailer tandems right in the ditch in the center of the road.

I had to force myself to just take a deep breath, calm down and tell myself that it was no big deal. There would be some place up ahead where I could pull off and get going back in the right direction. It would only cost me 10 or 15 minutes. And it does not take forty acres to turn a rig around.

'A' Type Driving Personality

When it comes to work, I have an 'A-type' personality. I do not like being slowed down by 'stupid' mistakes. I become possessed to get in as many miles each day as I can. I tend to push the envelope and come as close to the 11 hour driving limit as I can.

This led to several instances when I violated the 11 hour Rule by 5 or 10 minutes. It may not sound like such a big deal, but it began to take a big physical and psychological toll on me. It took me awhile to learn that all the stress and aggravation I was bringing on myself simply was not worth the few extra miles I gained.

I learned that planning to drive 10 hours, and then knowing exactly where I was going to spend the night based on my trip planning the night before or earlier that day, was the way to go. Trip planning is the key. Then just enjoy the ride. If something happens along the way, like unexpected traffic, issues with the truck, road closures, construction, etc., no problem. You know your route; you did your trip planning and know exactly what is coming up and where you can go.

It really is a pleasant job once you bring yourself to simply enjoy the drive and know that you will do whatever you can to get the load to its destination on time. If 'stuff' comes up that is out of your control, do your best to deal with it, communicate with your dispatcher, and 'truck on'. As I said before, being a truck driver is really a great job, once you get through the beginner jitters and doubts, and get a little experience under your belt.

In connection with this topic of performing good trip planning, I ran across a surprising violation I was unaware of, that you can be cited for during a roadside inspection. I am not sure how officials determine this, but in 2012 alone, there were 103 violations listed for: <u>Scheduling a Run to Necessitate Speeding</u>. In other words, they received a citation for not doing proper trip planning. They did not have enough hours to complete the trip without speeding.

CHAPTER 18

URINE BOTTLES/CONTAINERS AND WATER CONSUMPTION

Importance of Water Consumption

If you read any health publication on the issue of water, you will learn the importance of consuming plenty of water throughout the day. It is very important that you consume at least half your body weight, in ounces. So if you weigh 160 lbs., drink at least 80 ounces of water throughout the day. Here are some facts you may not have known about water: 1

* You need consume at least 64 ounces of water a day. Not consuming enough water places a lot of stress on your kidneys. 1
* You cannot depend on thirst to tell you when to drink. By the time the sensation of thirst kicks in, you already are slightly dehydrated. Drink regularly, even when you don't feel thirsty. This is especially true for adults over age 60, because the sensation of thirst is blunted in older people. 1
* Low level dehydration (a condition many people don't even know they have) is linked to: high blood pressure, irritability, depression, lack of focus, pain, stiff joints, muscle spasms, headaches, sugar and carbohydrate cravings, weight gain, indigestion, heartburn, constipation, and kidney stones. 1
* Water is the main source of energy in the body because it generates electrical and magnetic energy within every cell. Without water, noting lives. 1
* Water is the main solvent in the body. It is necessary for breaking down food into smaller particles for digestion and metabolism. Water increases the rate of nutrient absorption and is the solvent for the materials that dissolve in the blood and other fluids in the body. 1

* Water is the main vehicle for transporting substances throughout the body, including the elimination of toxins through the liver, kidneys, bladder, bowels, skin and lungs. 1
* Improved immunity is a big benefit of drinking plenty of water daily. 1
* Water is the main lubricant in the joints, spine, and eyes. Drinking enough water daily can help remove the accumulation of acid waste in joints, such as uric acid, which can cause inflammation and pain. It also can help prevent glaucoma in the eyes. 1
* Water also provides the necessary cushioning in the spinal discs. To me that is especially important with all the back problems I have. 1
* The human brain is about 80% water. Water gives the brain the electrical energy for all brain functions. Drinking plenty of water will help with better thinking and can help prevent attention deficit disorders like dementia, Alzheimer's, Parkinson's and Lou Gehrig's disease. 1
* Blood is about 85 to 95% water! So, when a person is dehydrated, the blood gets thick and sticky, making it more prone to clotting. Water helps remove toxins and fatty deposits from the arteries, which in turn reduces the risk of heart attacks and strokes. 1
* And finally, something that is important to all truckers, sleep. Drinking plenty of water can help improve sleep patterns and help reduce stress in the body. 1

Some trucking companies offer free information about how to check your urine to determine if you are consuming enough water. Your urine should be pale yellow. If it is dark yellow or tan colored, you are dehydrated and need to increase your daily water intake.

Urine Containers

With this in mind, one of the first things you need to get are two half gallon containers to relieve yourself when you need to pee, but are not near any facilities like a truck stop or rest stop. I recommend two because if you are drinking the amount of water you should be, one bottle fills up fast.

I purchased two half gallon plastic containers of apple juice because it had a wide opening, and a rigid plastic handle attached to the neck of the container. This rigid handle made it more secure to hold in place while I was in a seated position. Let me explain.

Usually I will pull off the road, stop the vehicle in a safe area, put on my 4 way flashers, and step into the sleeper berth to pee in the bottle. But on one or two occasions, I was stuck in traffic as a result of an accident that closed down the freeway. I had no place to pull off since the shoulder was being used by emergency vehicles. No one could move with all vehicles shut down, just waiting for the freeway to re-open. Even though my truck was completely shut down, I did not feel comfortable leaving the driver seat. So I grabbed my container while in the driver's seat, un-buttoned my pants, put my steering wheel all the way forward and up, and positioned the bottle so I could easily relieve myself.

I prefer the container with a handle around the neck as opposed to just holding onto the body of the container. The last thing you want to do is spill your pee bottle in the truck. With a handle around the neck of the container it is much easier to hold it securely with one or two fingers while you relieve yourself.

By the way, you should NEVER use your pee bottle while driving. Always find someplace to safely pull over.

In addition, I would not advise pulling your rig to the side of the road, jumping out of your truck and just urinating on the side of the road. Most, if not all jurisdictions have laws against urinating in public. So why subject yourself to an embarrassing citation, when there is a much better and more efficient way of taking care of this need to relieve yourself. Besides, you also unnecessarily open yourself up to a roadside inspection.

After relieving yourself while seated in the driver's seat, your *FIRST* act should be to place the container on the floor of the truck to the right of the driver's seat, <u>then</u> screw the lid back onto the container. DO NOT get distracted with zipping up/button up your pants and leaving your open urine bottle on the floor. Sure enough after buttoning up your pants, you will get distracted by something on the road, forget about your OPEN urine bottle and accidently knock over the container. You will then kick yourself for getting distracted and failing to put the lid back on the bottle as soon as you placed it on the floor of the truck cab. You will waste two days cleaning your truck floor. That urine smell is hard to get rid of. I never had an accidental spill, but I have been in trucks that have. Let me explain.

When I first started, I was instructed to go to the company yard in Denver and pick out my first truck. They had two trucks that were unassigned, so I was going to check them both out and pick the one I liked best. When I climbed into the first truck, I found it was a total mess. It had pizza boxes piled up on the floor, the strong smell of urine and it looked like someone had been sleeping in the back. It appeared someone was still living in this truck. It gave me the creeps. I could not get out of there fast enough.

Then I went to the second truck and it had that same strong smell of urine as well as chewing tobacco had been spit all over the dash board and steering wheel. The floor was all sticky and filthy. It was absolutely disgusting. But, since this second truck was the better of two evils, I spent the next several hours scrubbing out and cleaning this truck. I later learned just about every new driver goes through the same nightmare with their first truck.

Here is a strong suggestion to all 'break in' companies! When you have a driver who quits and leaves their truck at one of your facilities, take the damn time to have someone clean that truck out and detail it for the next driver. Show some respect for that new driver. Give that new driver a good first impression of your company, NOT the experience I had.

Now back to the topic; always remember to put the lid of your urine bottle back on immediately. Then you can take your time zipping up or buttoning up. I used to favor the military pants with the cargo pockets. Buy them a little bit large. Just buy one pair first to see if you like them; if you do then you can buy more.

Now, having mentioned the pre-caution above, that you should never try to pee in your bottle while you are actively driving the truck, some of you will do it anyway. So, let me set the stage.

If you are going to do that, you have to be aware that your attention has to be <u>completely</u> on the road. You have to discipline yourself to unbutton/ unzip your pants, put your steering wheel up and away, take the cap off and position the bottle so your penis is completely inside the bottle opening so you don't end up peeing all over yourself. You have to do all this while not letting your eyes leave the road. You have to make up your mind ahead of time that if something were to suddenly happen in front of the truck or you blow a steer tire or something similar, you will <u>immediately</u> drop your bottle, deal with the emergency in front of you, and clean up whatever mess there is later.

Your speed should be low, around 50 to 55 mph, and your cruise control should be set. There should be no vehicles for 1 mile in front of you.

Just to demonstrate how quickly things can happen, on my very first run from Denver to Salt Lake City. I was just outside Laramie, WY. It was dark, and a deer just 'appeared' in front of me. In this case I had no time to do anything. All I saw was the deer's shoulders and ears and heard a big bang at the same time. All I could do was hold the truck straight and not make any sudden movements. I had to clean off parts of the deer later down the road after I stopped for the night. My point here is you never know when something like that will happen, so you have to stay focused on the road in front of you at all times.

When it comes to emptying your bottles, I wait until I am near some empty field or pulled off the road to empty my bottle into the weeds or brush. If you are concerned about the smell from the bottle, as I was, there is a trick to mitigate that problem. Buy some Green Apple liquid hand soap (Wal-Mart) and squirt about a tablespoon into the bottom of your urine bottle. It will eliminate the odor of urine. You can also use liquid bleach, but some people hate the smell of bleach. Either way it completely mitigates the odor when you open the bottle.

Now let's talk about one other related topic. Have you ever been on the road or someplace where you were not near a restroom, and for whatever reason, you _suddenly_ need develop a case of diarrhea. It doesn't happen very often, but when it does, it can ruin your day. In my case it happened early in the morning while I was in my truck, getting dressed and preparing to start the day. I was very lucky, in that I happen to be staying at a rest stop, so I didn't have far to go. But even with the restroom being so close, I almost didn't make it in time. That near accident got me thinking that I had better have something available in the truck in case of those types of emergencies.

I researched various portable chemical toilets and settled on the 'Reliance Luggable Loo' (www.RelianceProducts.com), which is basically a 5 gallon bucket with a seat, plastic liners and chemicals that go into the plastic liner. I am so glad I bought that porta potty, because sure enough it happened two more times, with no restrooms within 20 miles. But I had set up my porta potty as soon as I received it, put in the liner and the dry chemical. I was prepared and I encourage you to do it as soon as you are hired by a company and setting up your first truck.

CHAPTER 19

TRIP PLANNING

Trip planning is simply calculating how long it will take you to drive from point A to point B. There are a number of factors you need to consider as you do your trip planning. I will only briefly go over this, as you will receive lots of training on this topic from whoever you work for.

While doing your trip planning, keep the process fairly systematic. First you will receive your pre-assignment, which is simply the first step the dispatcher takes in regards to your load. He will send you a pre-assignment, which basically gives you information on where you pick up the load, whether it is a live load (the shipper will load your empty trailer) or a drop & hook (you will drop your empty at the shippers lot, then hook up to a pre-loaded trailer) what the destination is, and how many miles it is between the two points.

When you review this information, go through your 'pre trip' process to determine if you can accept the assignment. You will look at how many hours you have you left on your DOT (Department of Transportation) 60/70 hour clock. You basically have 14 hours to get 11 hours of actual drive time in. Figure you can go 50 miles every hour, to account for traffic and necessary stops. If the trip is 600 miles, it will take you about 12 hours of actual driving time to reach your destination. Basically, if you have at least 16 hours of on-duty time left, you can safely accept the load. You DO NOT want to automatically accept a pre-assignment without going through the pre-trip process.

Part of the pre-trip process is looking at your *Motor Carriers' Road Atlas* and getting a bird's eye view of your route. When you receive your pre-assignment, you will also get a designated route from your navigation system. When I worked for Schneider, their navigation system automatically routed me on the most efficient route. These routes were sometimes not on the main inter-state highways, which is why you need to check your *Motor Carriers' Road Atlas*, to double check that the road you will be traveling on allows the type of vehicle you are driving and to insure there are no 'low clearance' bridges. I personally never had any problems with Schneider's navigation system, but you still need to check when you are driving on the less traveled designated highways. Driving on a highway and suddenly coming up to a bridge that is posted as being 12 feet high, will take the top of your trailer off if you attempt to drive under it, since your trailer is 13 feet 6 inches high. Every time you go under a bridge, take a quick look at the bottom of the bridge and chances are you will see evidence of someone who crashed into the bridge because the height his load exceed the maximum height of the bridge.

You need to study the *Motor Carriers' Road Atlas* and learn how to read a map so you can identify:

- Rest areas.
- Weigh stations.
- Time zones.
- Restricted routes.
- Where low clearance bridges might be on your route.
- How to locate and follow state designated routes for the type vehicle you are driving.
- How to calculate the total mileage between two points.
- How to quickly find the mileage between two cities within the same state.
- How to read the map legend.

CHAPTER 20

TEAM DRIVING

There is nothing good I can say about team driving. My opinion, as well as many others, is that people who team drive are truly risking their lives unnecessarily. The company makes a lot of profit from team drivers, but at a terrible cost to those drivers health.

I tried team driving once, and that was enough. It was one of the worst experiences of my life. I was so exhausted when I was driving; I was terrified I would fall asleep. I really don't know how I stayed awake. But that experience, along with information I gleaned from other team drivers convinced me that as a general rule, team driving is not safe.

When you team drive you become extremely fatigued. Basically it works like this; you drive 11 hours while your partner sleeps. Then your partner drives 11 hours while you sleep. That continues day after day, month after month. But you never get enough sleep, it is very difficult to get the kind of quality sleep your body needs, when the truck is moving. Your partner pulls into a truck stop to get fuel, you wake up. You get pulled into an inspection station, you have to wake up. You have a mechanical issue, you have to wake up. Your partner pulls into a rest area to go the restroom, you wake up. Your partner drifts off the highway and hits those wide groves or bumps that alerts you to the fact you are off the main road, you wake up. Your partner plays music, you wake up. You arrive at your destination to unload or pick up another trailer, you wake up. The simple movement and rocking of the truck interferes with getting sound sleep. The interruptions to your sound sleep are endless.

By the time it is your turn to take over the driving, you are dead tired from sleep deprivation. You are now driving extremely fatigued and if you are lucky enough to get through your 11 hours of driving, you then get to go back to bed, to be interrupted yet again as you try to sleep. This is not only a recipe for disaster when it comes to accidents, but this type of sleep deprivation that causes numerous serious medical problems. 1

Consistently getting good night's sleep isn't a luxury, it's essential to your health. Insufficient sleep not only leaves you feeling tired and irritable but also weakens your immune system and puts you at risk for depression, weight gain, chronic headaches, high blood pressure, heart disease, diabetes and even increases your risk of dying. 1

People with persistent sleep problems were three times more likely to die (of any cause) over a 19 year period, than those who got proper and adequate sleep. To get the full health benefits of sleep, most adults should aim for at least seven hours of <u>uninterrupted</u> sleep. 1

The bottom line is to avoid team driving. If you like to stay healthy and live, stay away from team driving. I have <u>heard</u> of some people that can sleep like a baby through all the distractions I have mentioned above. But every team driver I have ever actually <u>met</u>, admitted how tough it was and what a challenge it was to get enough rest while working on a team.

The only exception to team driving, where team driving actually makes sense, is if you team drive with your spouse. If they own their own truck and pick their own loads, they are not under the same pressure a company team is under to keep that truck rolling 24 hours a day. They can decide to drive 7 or 8 hours a piece and then sleep together, or drive whatever schedule they want. You have your spouse with you, so the issue of leaving your spouse at home for weeks at a time is a mute point. There is tremendous potential in traveling/ driving with your spouse <u>and</u> making a ton of money! When speaking with the wives that drive with their husbands I was very surprised how much they claimed to love it!

I met a few married couples who had no kids, or their kids were grown and on their own; some who had retired, and, like me were looking for a new adventure; who had taken up truck driving as a team to travel the U.S. and Canada, and get paid for it! Some spouses have told me they easily earn over 200,000 a year, and had trimmed their unnecessary expenses, increasing the amount of money they keep by 30 to 40%.

There was one couple who sold their home, and no longer maintained a permanent residence of any kind. If they need to lay up somewhere they either get a hotel or stay at a friends or relatives house, where they also store their personal vehicle. If they need a car out on the road, they simply rent one, like I did, using Enterprise car rental, because they will pick you up at the truck stop and drop you back off when you return the car. This couple has no mortgage, no rent, no car payments, no home insurance payments, no utility bills, no maintenance costs, no expenses normally attributed to maintaining a dwelling. They said they make a 'ton' of money.

Some people have told me they simply don't think they could live on the road like that. I thought the same thing at first. It is much easier than you think and driving a tractor and trailer actually grows on you after a short time. You begin to realize that a lot of the daily stresses you experienced at home or on a 'normal' job, simply don't exist on the road. Driving a truck is very liberating.

My recommendation is this. If a couple wants to dip their toe into this truck driving life style, first go to driving school together, get your commercial licenses, and then get hired by the same company.

All long haul companies are looking for team drivers. As I said before, a company makes more money off of team drivers because the truck is rolling almost all the time, carrying at least 80% more loads than a solo driver, over the same 30 day period.

When a solo driver reaches the end of his 11 hour maximum driving time, he must stop; take a minimum 10 hour break (sleep). After his required 10 hour break, he can then he can get back on the road. Where as a team will simply switch drivers, and keeps moving. The more loads a company can put in their trailers or flat beds, the more money it makes.

But first you <u>both</u> have to pass all your tests and evaluations to get hired. If one of you does not make it, fails one or more of the company evaluations, no problem. Don't have a cow or get all stressed out.

As your company runs you through the training, they will give you feedback on how you are doing and will tell you if you should be concerned about passing. Most companies will let you know if you should drop out, and start over in another future class. They will recommend you go back to a commercial driving school and get additional training in whatever area you are struggling in, then apply again. They do that because, if you fail the actual final 'on the road' evaluations, you cannot re-test for 6 months.

So, listen to their feedback and heed their advice. If one of you has to drop out because your simply not picking up on the material or are having a difficult time with shifting or backing or maneuvering the trailer correctly, then one of you may have to just move on and start driving while the other goes back to get additional training.

Eventually you will be together and can start your team driving adventure. Once you are together, it will not be easy. It may take a long time to adjust, but once you have gained more experience on the road, you will begin to see what I have been talking about.

You will be under pressure by the company to get your load to its destination as quickly as possible. You both have 11 hours of driving time to use up and they will expect you to use it to get that load to its destination in a timely manner.

After one year, if you are both in agreement to keep it going, you can start looking into programs the company may offer in regards to purchasing one of their used but good trucks, or getting a new truck on your own, and start picking your own loads, your own routes and setting your own schedule.

In the meantime, at .32 cents a mile, you should be able to earn <u>at least</u> $70,000 a year working as a team for any company.

Once you have your own truck, become an independent operator, earning from 90 cents to $2.00 or more a mile, you can easily start earning over $200,000 a year.

There is an excellent article on Team Driving in the Overdrive Magazine, August, 2013, page 24. Go to; <u>www.OverdriveOnline.com,</u> click on 'subscribe now' button located at the top right of the home page. You will then get the electronic version of this magazine FREE of charge. I have found it to be a good source of information. 2

CHAPTER 21

EXERCISES YOU CAN DO
WHILE DRIVING

Driving for long periods of time can absolutely ruin your back. Sitting for extended periods of time can lead to serious back ailments, not to mention blood clots in your legs that can lead to serious medical problems.

I am acutely aware of this since I have a very bad back condition.

In my case, in 1979, at age 28, I was involved in a very serious auto accident. I was very lucky to survive. Doctors told me I only survived because I was young and in very good physical condition.

Basically, I was ejected out the top of my Trans Am, which had removable glass T-Tops. I apparently (I have no memory of the accident) drove off a sharp curve on a mountain back road with a steep embankment. Just before going down the embankment, I clipped a tree which sent my car air born, flipping and spinning in the air.

I always wear my seat belt, but for some reason I must not have had it on in this instance, which ended up saving my life, as well as my buddy who was in the passenger seat. But, again I have no memory of at least 2 minutes prior to the accident. It is called retrograde amnesia. I only recall hearing what I later found out was my car falling to the ground after it hit the middle of a large 60 foot tree, about 30 feet off the ground. According to the Highway Patrol report the spinning action had so much force it shot me and my buddy out the top of the car. Our heads hit the glass T-Tops, (which they found intact, unbroken) which caused them to pop off, allowing both of us to be ejected.

Luckily my buddy had no injuries, a miracle. But I was not so lucky. Apparently I hit the steering wheel with such force I tore my spleen, collapsed my lung and fractured all my ribs. Then, as I was being ejected out the top, the rubber gasket that seals the T-tops hit me at the shoulder blades and ripped down my back as I was ejected.

The doctor advised me that my skin was the only thing that kept me from having all my back muscles ripped away from my body. My back muscles were apparently shredded and several of my transverse processes (the bones that stick out of each vertebra), on my spine were broken off.

I remember the car crashing down from where it had impacted the tall tree, with the cassette player still playing my Burton Cummings tape. The impact with the tree had crushed the entire driver side of the roof. I would have been dead had I not been ejected. I remember not being able to move or breathe very well.

At the time, I could not understand why I couldn't get up and climb up the embankment to the road. I ended up lying there, bleeding internally from a torn spleen and shredded back, slipping in and out of consciousness for over 7 hours. By the time my buddy was able to find help and get the ambulance to me I was close to death. I remember the ambulance medic instructing the driver to take a smoother route to the hospital or I may not make it.

The emergency room surgeons cut me open to repair what damage they could find and get 3 units of blood in me since I lost so much from all the internal bleeding.

Then they had to address my back, which by this time looked like I was 9 months pregnant. That took two additional back surgeries and 3 years to clear up. It took one year just to get my back muscles to stop bleeding. Doctors had to continually drain my back via a Hemovac medical device. This is a small round accordion like vacuum, with a tube inserted into my lower back. I wore this medical device to keep the blood from accumulating in my lower back. When it was all said and done, they ended up taking over 10 pints of blood out of my back before they could get it to stop.

If that wasn't enough, I was then advised I had chipped several transverse processes in my back, but they could not locate all the pieces. The doctors advised me that at least one of the bone pieces had sequestered itself somewhere in my back, possible next to my spinal cord. The doctors warned me that if that piece ever moves and impinges the spinal cord, it could paralyze me.

Around 1985 I had another accident while teaching at the police academy. I was thrown to the ground and landed awkwardly, which resulted in 2 ruptured discs. Eventually a neurosurgeon ended up taking out my L4 & L5 discs in 2000.

In addition, while working as an investigator, a drunk driver jumped the center divider and hit our undercover car <u>head on.</u> That accident really impacted my mid-back.

The reason I go into so much detail, is to emphasis that after all this, you can agree and clearly understand me when I say that I ended up with severe back problems. To this day my back muscles go into severe spasms whenever I am stressed or perform simple tasks like vacuuming a carpet or washing dishes.

So now, how could I possibly hope to drive an 18 wheeler for hours on end, every day, for weeks at a time? In addition, I still coach gymnastics. You would logically think, it would not be very likely.

Well my secret is doing back exercises and stretching every day. It really is as simple as that. Here is a sample of exercises that I did while actually driving the truck. These exercises will work with anyone.

Exercises 1 through 7 can be done while the vehicle is on cruise control, and on an open stretch of road with no traffic.

1.   Hip Flexor Exercise

The first exercise is designed to strengthen your hip flexors, which are a major source of back pain when they are weak and unbalanced. While sitting behind the steering wheel, adjust the steering column so that you can lift your knee about 4 to 6 inches off the floor before it makes contact with the bottom of the steering wheel.

Then while completely focusing on your driving, simply lift your knee straight up so it presses against the steering wheel. Press your knee against the bottom of the steering as hard as you can for at least 30 to 60 seconds. Then switch knees and do the same with the other knee.

Continue this until you have done at least 10 reps on each leg. You will find that as your hip flexor muscles become fatigued, your back will actually self adjust. You will feel your back begin to pop just like you were at the chiropractor. You will feel immediate relief in your back.

This is such a great, easy exercise. I learned this exercise from my chiropractor as she was treating me for my back problems. She had me sit in a chair and lift my knee up about 6 inches while I pressed down on my knee with my hands. I simply substituted the steering wheel of the truck for my hands.

2. Steering Wheel Press

This exercise works your chest and arms. With your left hand at the 9 o'clock position and your right hand on the 3 o'clock position, press your palms straight towards the middle of the steering wheel.

Press as hard as you can toward the center, like your trying to crush the steering wheel. Press for 30 to 60 seconds. Rest for 30 seconds and repeat. Complete 10 reps. There are two variations to this exercise. Do it with your arms completely straight and then with your elbows slightly bent.

3. Steering Wheel Pull

This exercise works the shoulders and back. With your hands in the same position as the steering wheel press, pull out on the steering wheel, pulling against your thumbs. Pull straight out for 30 to 60 seconds. Rest 30 seconds, then repeat. Complete 10 reps.

4. Steering Wheel Push-ups

This exercise works the triceps, back, shoulders and abdominal muscles. Position your hands on the steering wheel wherever they are comfortable, between 8 o'clock and 11 o'clock for the left hand and between 1 o'clock and 5 o'clock for your right hand. This exercise is best done under the same circumstances as the hip flexor exercise.

You should have the vehicle in cruise control and traveling on a long straight run with no traffic. Place both feet flat on the floor, engage your abdominal muscles (stomach) and crunch your chest toward the steering wheel while resisting with your arms. Once you get within a couple inches of the steering wheel, press yourself back to an upright position, while continuing to crunch forward as hard as you can to provide resistance against the arms.

Continue this just like you would if you were doing regular push-ups, but instead of your body weight and gravity providing resistance, you are using your abdominal muscles to provide the resistance.

Do as many as you can until your arms and abs just can't take any more. Rest 1 minute and repeat. Try to do 3 sets.

One of the cool side effects of these exercises is that if you were feeling lethargic and tired before doing these exercises, you will feel energized, wide awake and alert after.

5. Steering Wheel Chest Pulls

This exercise works the biceps, forearms, lower back and abdominal muscles. While seated, you can do this exercise with your hands in two different positions.

To work the biceps, position your hands on the bottom of the steering wheel, palms up. To work the forearms and biceps, position your hands at the 3 and 9 o'clock positions. With this exercise, like the hip flexor exercise, you need to be driving with the cruise control on, on a straight, long road with <u>no</u> traffic around and no vehicles in front of you for at least 1 mile.

Grab the steering wheel, pull the heels of your feet up against your seat, and pull your chest to the steering wheel, while trying to pull back with your back muscles the entire time. Straighten out to an upright position again, all the while pulling back with you back muscles. Do 30 to 60 reps. Rest 1 minute and repeat 2 or 3 times.

6. Running In Place While Seated

Sitting for prolonged periods is not good for your health. This exercise helps you address the negative effects of sitting for long periods, by getting your heart rate up while working your legs.

While driving with the cruise control on, on a straight road with no traffic, position both feet <u>flat</u> on the floor, knees spread as far apart as you can get them, lift one knee up as high as you can, then as you let that leg go back to the floor, lift the other leg as high as you can. Continue this as <u>fast</u> as you can, like your running in place, but your knees are the only part of your body moving. Go as fast as you can, alternating each leg until your legs become so fatigued, you can no longer lift your leg. Really push it. Remember to continue to keep your knees as wide as you can. Rest for 1 minute and repeat. Do 3 or 4 reps.

7. Deep Breathing

When we don't get enough oxygen in our system due to prolonged shallow breathing, our cells begin to suffer. Low oxygen levels in the body tissues are a sure indicator for disease. Lack of oxygen in the tissues is the fundamental cause for <u>all</u> degenerative diseases, and plays a large role in causing cells to become cancerous. 1

You may never know that your cells are being starved for oxygen, due to shallow breathing. You will simply feel the effects like headaches, lack of focus, memory loss, chronic pain, and constant fatigue. Over time these dying cells lay the foundation for heart failure, dementia and cancer. 1

More oxygen helps clear your mind, repairs your aging brain. Getting more oxygen into your cells can help wash away toxic heavy metals, chemicals, pesticides, and oxidized fats. When you expose bacteria, viruses and cancer cells to oxygen, they die. 1

This is a deep breathing exercise that can be done anywhere and anytime. This exercise helps calm you, refocus and exercise your lungs and diaphragm.

This breathing technique is one that I used while driving a truck. I originally learned this technique (among other breathing techniques) while studying Aikido and studying under Bob Koga. It is the one I used most often because of the versatility and flexibility of the technique.

First, breathe in through your nose to a count of 10. As you breathe in, imagine you have a balloon in your abdomen that you are trying to fill first, before your lungs. This utilizes and exercises your diagram, which is the key to all breathing.

Fill that balloon to capacity, and then expand your lungs. Once you have reached the count of 10 and breathed in as much as you can, try to cram a little more air in, hold for 10 seconds, and then breathe out your mouth.

As you breathe out, open your mouth and pretend your throat is a meter and you are controlling/ restricting the rate at which the air leaves your lungs. Count to 10 as you breathe out. When you reach the count of 10 and think you have emptied all the air from your lungs, once again engage your diaphragm as if you are doing a crunch sit up and squeeze every last molecule of air from your lungs. This helps get all that 'stale' air out of your lungs and really exercises the diaphragm.

During shallow breathing, which is what you do most of the day, much of the air in your lungs never leaves your lungs and becomes stale.

The remaining exercises are done when you are not driving, or someone else is driving, and you are in the sleeping berth.

8. Plank

The plank is a great way to strengthen your core muscles which are extremely important for professional drivers.

Sitting behind the wheel of a truck all day can lead to a bad back in no time at all.

There are a couple variations to this exercise. Let's start with the easy one first. Simply lie down in your bed in the truck, on your stomach. Put your elbows under you, about shoulder width apart, prop yourself up so your body is straight, up on your toes. Hold that position for at least 60 seconds.

The other variation to this is doing it with your arms straight, in a push up position. This does double duty in that is works your arms as well as you core muscles.

9. Straight Arm Plank Rowing

This exercise is my favorite. It does double duty in that it gives you all the benefits of the plank as discussed above and adds the shoulders and arms. Start with a set of dumb bells, whatever weight you can handle.

Get down on your hands and knees and then grab the dumb bells, one with each hand. Get yourself in a push-up position over the weights, hands about shoulder width apart.

From this position pull the weight straight up, keeping your elbow close to your side, until it is almost touching your hip or waist area. Then put the weight back down and lift the other weight in the same manner.

Complete as many as you can, rest 60 seconds and then do a second set.

When you first try this you may have to spread your feet out wide in your push-up position in order to give you more stability. But as you get stronger, start to bring you feet closer together to engage your core muscles even more.

10. Exercises While Stopped at a Road Side Rest Area

I sometimes would pull off into a nice rest stop, and do 15 minutes of intense exercises utilizing the picnic tables and any hills located on the grounds.

Hill Sprint—Find a small hill and sprint up the hill as fast as you can. Then turn around and walk down. As soon as you reach the bottom, immediately turn and sprint back up. Continue this until you complete at least 5 sprints.

Step-Ups—Find a picnic table or bench that is about 18 inches off the ground. With your right leg, step up on the low bench area of the picnic table until your leg is straight, then lift your heel off the surface as far as you can, extending up on your toe. Your lower left leg will be straight and lifted back behind you slightly. Then lower yourself until your left foot touches the ground, at which point you will immediately press down on your right foot again, stepping up on that right foot/leg.

This is like doing 15 consecutive leg presses with your right leg. Just step up like you're climbing a big stair case, but only using your right leg, with you left leg straight behind you, pointing toward the ground and helping you balance.

Then switch and do 15 with your left leg. Rest for 30 to 60 seconds and repeat.

On the second set you will probably not be able to do 15 reps, just do as many as you can.

Bar Dips—Using the same bench, grab the edge of the bench or picnic table seat; stretch your legs out straight. Sit so that your tail bone clears the edge of the bench while grabbing the edge of the bench.

Bend your elbows and lower yourself down as far as you can. Do as many dips as you can. On this exercise you do not want your tail bone or lower back scraping on the edge of the bench as you bend your elbows and lower yourself down. The constant rubbing and scrapping can lead to calcium build up on those bones impacted.

Rest for 30 to 60 seconds, then do another set of dips, as many as you can.

Straddle "V" Leg Raises—Sit on the bench, grab the rear of the bench, lean back, resting your upper back on the picnic table top. Start by spreading your feet as far apart as you can, with your heels on the ground. Then bring your straight legs up together in front of you, getting your feet as high as you can, until you are in a "V" position.

Then lower them to the starting point, spreading your feet as wide as you can get them, with the heels just coming to within one inch of the ground, then power them back up in front of you, feet together, back to the "V" position. Do as many as you can. Usually just do one set and move on to the next exercise listed below.

Arch or 'Half Circle" Leg Raises—Maintaining the same seated position as the straddle "V" Leg raises, but this time stretch both legs out in front of you, keeping both feet together on the ground all the way to your right, as far as you can but still keeping both heels on the ground.

Now pull both feet up in a arch or half circle so by the time they get directly in front of you they are at their highest point, and continue none stop until both feet are as far to the left as you can get them, but stop when they are about one inch from the ground.

Keep tracing this half circle/ arch with your feet glued together switching from right to left and back to right, like a windshield wiper.

Keep going until your abdominal muscles can't take any more. After resting 30 to 60 seconds, complete one more set of the straddle V leg raises, rest, and one last set of the arch/half circle leg raises.

Sideways Butterfly Kicks—While maintaining the same seated position described above, hold your legs straight in front of you, about 2 feet off the ground. Separate your feet about 12 inches. Now, scissor your feet, right over left, separate them 12 inches, then scissor them again, left over right. Repeat this alternating scissoring action as fast as you can until you can't do any more. Do 2 sets.

Hop Overs—While standing next to a low and narrow fixed object, like a low pipe or low piece of playground equipment, like the one pictured below, grab the stationary object, lean forward and hop over it and back again. Repeat as many times as you can. See illustration below.

By the time you are finished, you feel refreshed, sharp and ready to hit the road.

Stress is a component of every job, even truck driving. Getting regular exercise is a good way to help combat this stress.

Recent research out of Tel Aviv University published in the Journal of Occupational Health Psychology, shows that the on the job stress can increase a person's risk of developing Type 2 diabetes. They found that those with large amounts of occupational stress, separate from other risk factors, were 18 percent more likely to develop Type 2 diabetes.

So it is to your benefit to eat well, and exercise to help you deal with whatever stress you may experience on a daily basis.

Remember, the new DOT physical standards are rightfully targeting those physical ailments and diseases that may impact your ability to safely drive a commercial vehicle. So take this seriously.

As I mentioned in a previous chapter, a new regulation went into effect on 7/1/2013, which mandated a 30 minute break for all commercial drivers, after they have been on duty for 8 hours. Now there is no excuse not to take your break at a nice rest stop and get at least 20 minutes of exercise.

CHAPTER 22

BASIC VITAMIN AND SUPPLEMENT INFORMATION

As a truck driver, it is going to become more and more difficult to qualify as a truck driver and to continue to renew your commercial driver's license with the ever increasing U.S. Department of Transportation rules, regulations and guidelines.

DOT is beginning to look real close at those drivers with serious disorders like diabetes, cardiovascular diseases, obesity, and any condition that would make them a potential risk as a commercial driver. DOT is beginning to look at any commercial driver with any serious medical problem as a risk.

Slowly they will begin to weed out those drivers with serious medical conditions that in any way could affect their driving. So, as you can see, taking care of yourself, living a healthy lifestyle is going to be a requirement as opposed to just something you should do.

Regardless of what your occupation is, getting proper and adequate nutrition is important. As professional drivers, it is difficult, at best, to eat as well as you should. So supplementation with vitamins, minerals and herbs is essential.

Below I will share the information I have gathered over the years and valuable web sites so you can do your own research in determining what is right for you. This information I provide is concise and brief, but will provide all you need to know to do your own research so you can make intelligent and informed decisions in regards to supplementation.

Warning: *Always check with your doctor before proceeding upon any regimen of vitamin and herbal supplementation or exercise program. Some herbs can interfere with or alter certain medications you may currently be taking. Sometimes these effects can be life threatening. So check with your doctor and your pharmacist before taking any supplements*.

All people who are trying to improve their mental and physical condition need to consider getting serious about stress reduction and getting some mild exercise. Stress reduction helps reduce pain.

You can engage in meditation, yoga and massage. Mild exercise, such as swimming and yoga, promotes circulation within the joints and will reduce inflammation and pain. Again check with your doctor before beginning an exercise program to insure that you are doing the proper exercises suitable for your particular circumstances.

Driving a truck can be rough on your body. I don't recall meeting a single truck driver that was not dealing with some kind of pain from a variety of ailments. From doing a lot of reading I have found numerous natural foods that not only fight pain, but some work better than drugs.

Joint Pain/Osteoarthritis:

Some of the best foods for this are Bing cherries, ginger, avocado oil and soybean oil. A study in the Journal of Nutrition, found Bing cherries, about 2 cups a day, had an 18 to 25 percent drop in C-reactive protein in their blood, a sign of inflammation. Bing cherries contain flavonoids, which are plant based compounds with antioxidant properties that lower inflammation.

When I can't find fresh cherries, I buy 'Tart Cherry Juice'. This is pure juice from cherries. One large bottle contains 325 cherries.

Ginger also contains strong anti-inflammatory agents that can reduce joint pain. Take about one to two teaspoons of ground fresh ginger every day. I would mix it into my oatmeal. You should experiment with it until you find something that works for you.

Avocado oil and soybean oil contain ingredients that reduce inflammation and cartilage damage in arthritis patients.

Boswellia serrata—This herbal remedy contains nutrients that reduce inflammation and improve both acute and chronic joint pain. Typical dose is 300 mg, three times a day for four weeks, then 300 mg one to three times a day if needed for pain.

Supplements that Sharpen your Memory :

Vitamin D—Most Americans do not get enough sunshine to manufacture sufficient vitamin D to meet their daily needs. Vitamin D is essential for bone strength as well as preventing some cancers. But what is new is that vitamin D appears to help the immune system remove *beta-amyloid*, an abnormal protein from the brain. Beta-amyloid causes the 'tangles' that are associated with Alzheimer's disease. Brain cells use vitamin D for learning, memory and other cognitive functions. It also is an antioxidant that protects neurons from cell damaging inflammation.

Fish Oil—The omega-3 fatty acids in fish oil supplements can improve your mood as well as your memory and other cognitive functions. A large portion of the brain consists of docosahexaenoic acid (DHA), one of the main omega-3's in fish oil. The brain uses DHA to form cell membranes. People who consume fish oil have better brain functions, including a faster transmission of nerve signals and improved blood flow to the brain. Try to get a proper ratio of one part omega-3 to every three parts of omega-6. Omega-6 is found in red meats, cooking oils, etc.

Multivitamin—As stated above, most truck drivers do not eat properly. So a good multivitamin, especially one that includes B vitamins, is good insurance and can help your brain. B vitamins nourish the myelin layer that covers brain cells. Studies have shown that people who do not get enough vitamin B-6 and B-12 and folic acid, tend to have the greatest declines in memory and other cognitive functions.

Vinpocetine—This comes from the periwinkle plant, and is able to cross the blood-brain barrier and improve brain circulation. It improves the oxygenation of the brain, especially when used in combination with other brain boosting supplements.

Ginkgo—This herb dilates blood vessels and reduces the 'stickiness' of platelets which are cell like structures in the blood that increase the risk for clots.

Ginkgo contains flavonoids as well as terpenoids, which are strong antioxidants that prevent damage to brain cells. There is strong evidence that ginkgo also improves memory and helps reduce the risk for vascular dementias and possibly Alzheimer's disease.

In order to organize the supplements you do take, I found it very helpful to get three of the largest full week pill box/containers you can find at any large drug store. They are labeled every day of the week, are large enough to fit all your supplements and the lids to each compartment lock in place. I take a lot of supplements, about 12 different ones, so I need the largest container they had. This way I don't waste time every morning having to open each bottle to remove one capsule. I have it all set up for 3 weeks at a time. I put one supplement, like ginkgo, in each of the 7 compartments (or 21 in my case since I set up 3 weeks' worth of vitamins). I continue this until I have all my supplements in each compartment. Then I just have to open the Monday compartment and pour all my supplements for that day into my hand. I then place them in a little change cup on my dash right in front of me, within easy reach, and take half around mid-morning and the rest around 3:00 pm. It is a big time saver.

Improve Energy and Alertness:

Protein—When you have been behind the wheel for a few hours, your energy level naturally drops off. Instead of reaching for that sugar laden 'energy' drink, research shows that it is protein, not sugar, that stimulates the cells we rely on to help us fight fatigue. According to research, they studied the effect of several nutrients on 'orexin cells', which secrete stimulants in the brain that cause us to expend energy and stay awake. The number of nerve impulses generated by orexin cells were increased by the intake of amino acids (building block of proteins) similar to those found in egg whites and nuts. Whereas glucose, a sugar, blocked these impulses.

Super Foods:

There are some foods that are considered 'super foods' because they contain an amazing source of a variety of nutrients in their best form. Here is a brief list; but do your own research on which ones might be for you: Cacao Powder; Sweet Potatoes; Maca Root powder; Organic Coconut Palm Sugar; Liquid Chlorophyll; Coconut Water; Chia Oil or Seeds; Raw Unfiltered Honey; Tamari Almonds; Acai Berry; Dulse leaf; Wakame; Seaweeds; Noni juice; Spirulina & Chlorella (www.amazinggrass.com/ www.macrolifenaturals.com/, www.Elmag.com/supergreens).

Earthing

This is a fairly new health discovery that was passed onto me by a trusted friend. The concept centers around re-connecting with the earth. When I first heard about this, my first thought was, oh no, not more new age, tree hugging crap. But my source was a very health conscious, intelligent and grounded individual who has never steered me wrong.

I learned it from Sensei Robert Koga as he was battling lung cancer. He used grounding sheets to help him sleep better and ease a lot of his aches and pains as he battled his cancer. I respected his opinion, so I elected to try it.

The results were almost immediate. I immediately started to sleep through the night, which I rarely do. My wife also noticed she began to sleep much better, so she became an instant fan of the grounding sheets.

I have been recently having severe pain in my wrists and thumb joints. The pain is so bad that I often cannot even open a jar, tear open a bag of chips or open a box of cereal. I could not even write down someone's phone number, as the slightest pressure on my thumb joint caused me to just drop the pen I was trying to write with. All those pains were mitigated at least 70% to 80% within one week of sleeping on the fitted sheet, grounded to the outlet next to my bed. I would not have believed it if I had not personally experienced it.

I did more research and read the book, "Earthing" by Dr. Stephen Sinatra, M.D., Clinton Ober and Martin Zucker, and am gaining a much better understanding of what is happening to me and why. It is absolutely fascinating and I highly encourage you to do your own research into this ground breaking information. Go to: www.earthing. com and I hope it helps you as much as it has helped me. I would not have added this information to this book if I had not personally experienced and benefited from the concepts surrounding this phenomenon. Some people believe that this is the most important health discovery ever! The concept is pretty simple. It is a fast growing movement based upon the major discovery that connecting to the earth's natural energy is foundational for vibrant health.

I am now a believer in the grounding technology. My recommendation to you is to visit the web site, and review the information, watch the video clips of the stories of persons who have benefited from this technology and try it for yourself.

I started grounding after I stopped driving. There are several ways you could benefit from this information while on the road. First is to simply follow the principles of grounding, by walking bare foot on the grass for 20 minutes while you are on your mandatory breaks.

As much as this product has helped me, I would find a way to park my rig directly next to a grass area so I could plug in the grounding rod and run the wire up into the sleeper. I remember many of the rest stops I took my mandatory 10 hour break at had parking spots that you could park parallel to the grass area between the rest stop and the highway. So if you want to start trying the product in your sleeper, start looking for grass areas where you can park your rig next to and get grounded while you sleep.

CHAPTER 23

WINTER DRIVING TIPS

Windshield Wipers

One of my first really scary moments was during my first trip in snowy, icy slush conditions from Denver to Salt Lake City. Whenever a truck would pass me, which was all the time since my truck was governed so I could only go 62 mph; the trucks wheels would send a dirty, icy slush onto my windshield and literally blind me.

My windshield wipers were not up to the task of handling that kind of material, and my windshield wiper fluid was only dribbling out. I might as well of been driving with my eyes closed. It scared the hell out me.

I somehow got off the road and had to hand wash my windshield with paper towels and Windex. I fixed my windshield wipers after discovering the sprayer had slipped down the frame of the wiper. I pulled the spraying mechanism back up the frame of the windshield wiper then secured it in place with a small plastic tie. I also used an old tooth brush to clean the surface of the spray head. It worked perfectly after that.

Make sure, long before winter arrives, to check that your windshield wipers are in good condition and fill up with winter wiper fluid. Most companies will have their own winter blend of wiper fluid at their operating centers. Fill up there every chance you get. You should also carry a couple half gallons in your truck if you run low out on the road.

In addition, before you approach any metropolitan area, make sure you stop and clean all your outside mirrors.

I had one incident where I was coming down into Salt Lake City on a snowy day and did not realize that my mirrors had really caked up with muddy slush in just a few miles. Now I had to make lane changes to take my exit, but I couldn't see what was in the lane next to me. I was really scared. All I could do was begin my lane change real slow and listen for any cars honking that might be next to me.

I grew to really hate winter driving. Between the stress from driving in hazardous conditions, seeing other trucks crashed on the side of the road, the icy roads, the inability to see traffic clearly, other truckers driving like idiots. It was not fun.

Ice on the Air and Electrical Lines of the Trailer

Another unpleasant surprise during the winter was on a trip through eastern Colorado in December. It had just begun to snow; it was half snow half frozen slush. Once I got to the distributor's warehouse in Pueblo, I got out, walked to the back of my trailer to remove my lock and slide the tandems back.

I then noticed that the air and electrical lines at the rear of the trailer were caked with ice. The weight of the ice had stretched the springs and allowed the air and electrical line lines to drag on the ground. One wire was completely severed and one air hose was badly damaged. If that air hose had been cut, my trailer brakes would have locked up, which is a dangerous situation when driving in icy conditions.

This is a situation that had never been mentioned during any training, and was not covered in any book.

My point here is that there are so many things that can happen out on the road, they all can't possibly be covered in any one book or a training session. As they repeated several times in my initial training, "We can only tell you so much. Take what we teach you and the rest you will have learn as you go." Now I know what they meant.

So my message is, make sure you check those air lines on your trailer often when driving in icy conditions. I know it's a hassle to stop and check these items, but if you don't, and something goes wrong, like an air hose being severed, on an icy road, well I just hope you survive the resulting crash, and I hope innocent people are not injured or are killed as a result of your accident. Those are the type of things that will haunt you the rest of your life; emotionally, financially and legally.

Tire Chains

Tire Chains, ah yes, I hate tire chains. So, let me touch on what I did to lessen my apprehension about putting on truck tire chains.

Every experience I have had with putting on tire chains on a passenger vehicle has been a bad experience. So, faced with the prospect of putting chains on a tire 3 times the size of the tire on my car, and weighing about

40 lbs. each, I was not looking forward to it. So, I decided to mitigate my fears by facing this daunting task head on.

As soon as you get your truck assigned to you, check to make sure you have all the chains and cables you are required to have. When I got my initial truck, I checked the 'chain box' near the rear wheels and found about 3 old and rusty tire chains. They also had broken and missing links. If I had not checked and got into a situation where I needed to use those chains, I would have been in a world of hurt, not to mention a possible citation for not having operational chains available. So I immediately went to the shop and advised the mechanic of my situation. He threw the old chains in a huge pile of other old rusty chains, and gave me the proper number of new chains and cables.

When the weather is nice, I recommend practicing putting your tire chains and cables on. You do not want to be that driver that waits until it is freezing cold, and is driving up a mountain pass that is requiring all trucks to put on chains, and you have no idea how to do it. If you have not done it at least two times, you will be in for one of the worst experiences of your life. It will be cold and wet, with other trucks and cars driving by, splashing you with cold, wet slush, while you are struggling to figure out how to put these 40 lb. chains on.

I met a fairly new driver who was working at one of the operating centers, that was on disability because a car hit him while he was putting his chains on.

Most chain stations/pull-outs have a 30 minute time limit to get your chains on and get back on the road. You are not the only person trying to get chains on and there are a lot more trucks behind you that also need to put their chains on. So the State or Highway Patrol will often monitor these chain stations, in order to keep trucks moving through quickly. If you take too long, they can and will cite you.

They are also checking to insure truckers are putting on the required number of chains, depending on which state you are in. Be familiar with the number of chains and their specific placement as required for each state you will be traveling through. In the winter survival book you should be getting from whatever company you decide to work for, you will find about 10 states that have chain requirements, and they are all different. Some states require only two chains, one on each outside drive wheel, and some require up to six chains on the eight drive wheels and two on the trailer tires. Here is a quick summary:

Arizona—No requirements but, they do recommend at least two of the outside front drive wheels be chained. They have no requirements for the trailer.

California—This state has the most stringent requirements. All four tires on the front drive axle must be chained as well as both outside wheels of the rear drive axel. In addition, they require chains on the outside of either trailer axel. Good luck getting those chains on those inside drive tires.

Colorado—This state requires link type chains on the outside wheels of either drive axel and cable type chains on the outside wheels of the other drive axel. No chains on the trailer are required.

Idaho—This state requires chains on the outside of each of the drive axel wheels and chains on any two of the outside trailer tires.

Michigan—This state not only has no chain law, but it is illegal for trucks to use tire chains in this state. I am assuming they don't want the trucks tearing up their road surfaces.

Montana—This state requires all four tires of the front/primary drive axel be chained. Again, good luck with those inside drive tires. Also, there is no requirement for chains on any of the trailer tires.

Nevada—This state requires chains on any two of the outside drive axels and chains on any two of the outside tires on the trailer.

Oregon—This state requires chains on all four wheels of the front/ primary drive axel and chains on either of the outside tires on the trailer.

Utah—This state requires chains on either of the outside tires of the front/primary drive axel and no requirements for chains on the trailer.

Washington—This state requires chains on the outside tires of both drive axels and only one chain on a outside tire of the trailer.

Wyoming—This state requires only one chain on each of the outside tires of the primary drive axel.

This is a brief summary of some of the chain laws. These laws may have changed recently, so double check. Putting chains on and taking them off is probably the worst duty you will have to endure. Most of the drivers I spoke with indicated that if the roads are so bad they are requiring chains, they pull over and wait.

I was introduced to a cool little trick by an old truck driver, which allows you to put your chains on without having to pull forward or back over the chains to get them positioned correctly.

If you have ever put chains on or have seen it done, you know you usually drape the chain over the tire, then drive over the excess, stop, and the wrap the chain around and fasten the ends together. Or lay the chains out flat, drive over them, then pull them over the tire and secure. If you have done it, you know it is not that easy and things don't always go smoothly. The chains never go on as easy as the directions lead you believe they should. Sometimes it can get so bad you just feel like climbing back into your vehicle and crying.

The trick this driver showed me involved a piece of 4x4 lumber, cut at about a 25-degree angle. This acted like a wedge or ramp. He placed the cut 4x4 wedge/ramp under the <u>inside</u> drive wheel on each side. He pulled forward or backward depending on where the wedge was placed, and ended up lifting all the rear tires up off the ground a few inches as he drove up the wedge. This allows you to drape the chains over the top of the tire and then just pulling the excess under the tire, eliminating the extra step of having to get back into the truck and pulling up to drive over the chain.

If you have ever done this, sometimes it takes two or three tries to get the tire and chain in the correct position. This little trick eliminates all those steps. Remember to put the wedge/ramp under the inside drive tire or you have accomplished nothing, because the wedge/ramp will be blocking your ability to just slip the chain under the tire.

I went a little more heavy duty and built my wedge/ramp out of three pieces of 2x6 lumber, treated with a waterproof sealer. My base piece was made of a piece of 2x6 about 18 inches long. I then attached the next 2x6 piece, about 15 inches long, on top, with the back ends flush. I fastened the two pieces together with 6 inch deck screws (6 screws), screwed in from the top through the 15 inch pieced and through the base piece so that about 2 inches of the screw was exposed through the bottom of the base 18 inch piece. I wanted the screws to extend out the bottom of the base piece in order to grip the snow and ice as I began to drive up the wedge and prevent the wedge from slipping on the snow/ice. I then put on one more 2x6 piece, about 12 inches long, flush with the back, so all three ends are flush with each other. I would then fasten it with four 4 inch deck screws. Make sure all the screws are recessed into the wood about 1/8th an inch. This would give me a 12 inch flat platform on top to drive on to, giving me about 4 to 5 inches of clearance to pass that chain under.

Obviously, you need to <u>set your brakes</u> and <u>turn your engine off</u> while outside wrestling with the tire chains. Also, if you are putting chains on, you should already have locked in all four drive wheels for better traction. Remember to read and follow all your companies' directions for properly installing the tire chains or cables they provide.

Slow Down on Ice & Snow

While driving in winter conditions, I saw so many truck accidents where it was obvious excessive speed for the conditions was a contributing factor. It was amazing to me how many truck drivers drive their truck & trailer like it's a sports car.

Besides Schneider drivers, I only saw a hand full of trucking companies' that drove safely during inclement weather on a <u>consistent</u> basis, i.e., J.B.Hunt, Heartland, Pride, Stevens Transportation and a few others I just can't remember. There is no need to point out who the worst drivers are, that will be obvious once you get out on the road.

The most important advice I can give you is to slow down and <u>increase</u> following distances during <u>any</u> inclement weather. It's a simply rule, but a rule that will help you stay out of a lot of trouble.

While I was driving through early morning traffic in Chicago, it was obvious the freeway had a few patches of ice remaining that you couldn't see, but you could sure feel the ice patches as well as see other cars in front of you that were losing traction. Most of the traffic was going really slow as a result of the ice, except for one stupid tanker driver who was going too fast in the middle lane. Sure enough he had to brake for traffic in front of him, he lost traction, and his tanker jack-knifed and took out two cars. What an idiot! But you will see a lot of these drivers out there. Just stay as far away from them as you can. Don't get sucked into their mistakes.

5th Wheel and WD-40

During the cold winter months the moving parts of the fifth wheel, the locking mechanism and pivot points, do not operate smoothly and can freeze up. Please take the time to spray WD-40 into the locking assembly and on the pivot points that allow the fifth wheel platform to pivot down toward the trailer. If that locking mechanism of the fifth wheel does not close properly on the king pin, eventually that trailer will separate from your truck.

If that trailer is full and at maximum weight (40 tons for truck & trailer) and you are traveling 65mph on a freeway filled with families heading out on vacation and the trailer separates. Picture it, and just remember it can easily happen to you. So it is critical you follow the directions and training you will be getting when you go to the company training.

Make sure you push the locking handle in and check there is no gap between the trailer and fifth wheel. Use a <u>bright</u> flashlight to check under the trailer to insure the locking bar is completely across the king pin. There are additional steps, but I am only highlighting the ones I found critical and easily missed.

Bunk Heater

Since I am talking about winter tips, I should address the bunk heater used to heat your sleeping area during those freezing nights, and I mean freezing. The nights up north can get extremely cold and your bunk heater has to be operating correctly in order to be comfortable at night. As soon as you get your truck assigned to you, read the manual on the bunk heater. <u>After</u> reading the manual and any instructional material the company provides, test the heater out to insure it is operating correctly. You do not want to wait until you need it, to find out it doesn't function properly. It may take a week or two before you can get it into the shop. In the meantime you will be freezing at night. Many of the states have statutes limiting idle time, so idling the truck engine and running the truck heater is often not an option. The local and state police can and will issue a citation for idling beyond the allowed time.

The idling statutes were primarily enacted to deal with pollution created by thousands of idling trucks. Some states are very serious and strict about these laws. So avoid the entire mess by doing a pre-winter systems check. Obviously when the temperatures are really cold, like minus 10, most companies will require you to idle your engine all night.

Also be aware that many companies offer you quarterly bonuses based on several criteria, such as averaging at least 12 miles per gallon, not speeding, staying on the recommended route, fueling when and where they recommend and keeping your idle time under a specific limit. The company will have specific exemptions where idling will be allowed, but just be aware, excessive idling can disqualify you from receiving your quarterly bonus.

When I use the bunk heater in my truck, I not only close the windshield shades, but I also close the heavy shades that closes off the bunk area from the driver area. This gives you a smaller area to heat and is easier for the heating unit to keep your bunk area warm.

When I first used my bunk heater I made the mistake of placing some cloths on the floor, right in front of the heater vent. About an hour later,

I was curious why the bunk area was not heating up. I was not aware exactly where the vent was, so when I reached down along the floor to check where the heater vent was, I found that the cloths I had placed on the floor were blocking the heating vent. I was shocked how damn hot those cloths got. So, Make sure you don't block the heater vent with anything.

I found that 65 to69 degrees was a perfect temperature to set your heater during the night. Then, about an hour before I get up, I would turn the heater up to the maximum, pull the divider curtains back so the driver portion of the cab is open. Then I go back to sleep. By the time I am ready to get up, the entire cab is nice and warm. It is much more pleasant to be able to get dressed, get whatever paperwork done, start my pre-trip, check for messages, all in a nice warm cab. Be aware that once you start you truck engine, your cab heater will automatically turn off.

Recommended Winter Items

These are a few of the items you need to make sure you have in your truck before winter hits:

1. A good cold weather sleeping bag and warm blankets. If your truck stops operating and you are stuck in a snow storm where no one can get to you, be prepared.
2. Insulated work boots. If you have to spend any extended time outside, you will be glad you have these on.
3. Insulated work gloves. Sweeping a trailer out in cold weather is no fun, so be prepared.
4. A pair of insulated coveralls. If you have to put chains on, you will be crawling on the ground, getting wet and dirty. If you have some sort of break down that requires you to be outside in the cold for any length of time, you will want these on. When you finish, you will want to shed whatever you were wearing and get clean dry clothes on. These insulated coveralls are easy to put on and take off.
5. A really warm hat that covers your ears. I got one of these Russian style hats from a truck stop that really worked well. A full face ski mask works well too.
6. Candles, matches, and empty coffee cans that you can place your candles in. In case you are broken down for an extended

period, in a storm and no one can get to you for hours, these items will come in handy if your truck will not start.

7.   In connection to #6 above, keep some kind of emergency food in your truck. This can be candy bars, various types of nuts, power bars, bottle water, canned goods, canned drinks etc.

CHAPTER 24

TRUCK DRIVER SHORTAGE

According to USA Today, as of July 2011 there was a shortage of qualified and experienced truck drivers. The shortages are delaying some deliveries of products and raw materials, raising freight costs. According to the article some freight companies had to offer $10,000 bonuses to entice new drivers.

Despite some stagnation in available freight and driver lay-offs due to the recession, an increased demand for truck drivers will be driven by a reduction in the number of existing drivers resulting from both more stringent safety regulations and an aging driver population.

The American Trucking Association predicts a moderate increase in freight, which will further fuel the driver shortage problem.

Reuter's news agency reported that an analyst with logistics consultancy firm, FTR Associates, predicts a driver shortage of about 500,000 in 2012, as the recovering increases demand and new regulations crimp supply. The number of drivers retiring due to age or the new safety regulations will likely be the biggest contributor to the truck driver shortage.

More recently, according to the American Trucking Association, for the 1st quarter of 2013, the driver turnover rate at large truckload fleets was 97%. At small truckload fleets, the turnover rate was 82%. I was amazed the figures were that high. 1

Just prior to publishing this book I received an internet notice of a new article addressing the latest information on the driver shortage in the trucking industry, especially in the energy sector, involving tanker drivers. 1

The U.S. Energy Information Administration stated that oil delivered to refineries by truck increased by 38 percent between 2011 and 2012. The need for tanker drivers is booming, but there simply are not enough qualified drivers to fill the need. Many of the tanker drivers (as well as other truck drivers) are approaching retirement and leaving the industry. As the energy sector begins to grow, there will not be enough drivers to fill the need, creating a huge shortage. 1

There are currently about 3 million truck drivers, but there is a need for at least 300,000 more. To add to this problem is the fact that the current turnover rate among truck drivers is <u>97 percent</u>, with some figures putting the turnover rate as high as 109 percent. 1

With increasing drivers retiring, stricter medical standards for drivers and increasing regulation on the entire industry, carriers will have to dramatically increase pay and home time to attract quality people, who can pass the medical exam and background check. Some articles are predicting the current shortage of 20,000 drivers may jump to 111,000 by 2014.

In order to get the latest information about the truck driver shortage, type "Truck Driver Shortage" or "Commercial Truck Driver Shortage", in the search bar.

CHAPTER 25

WIVES OF TRUCKERS AND WOMEN IN TRUCKING

I would be remiss if I did not address the wives or girlfriends of those of you who are contemplating jumping into a career of driving a Big Rig. One of the most difficult parts of being a new truck driver is being away from your wife or girlfriend and family. This includes those adorable pets that are often considered part of the family.

I remember my first trip home after being gone for four weeks. My wife said our two small dogs would search all over the house for me and would start to cry and whine when they couldn't find me. From the reports I was getting, they were very depressed. When I came home, these two small dogs (Shih Tzu/Maltese mix and a Bichon Frise) charged me as I came in the house and literally knocked me down. They would not stop jumping all over and licking me as I lay helpless on the carpet. Needless to say they were very happy to see me. This scene was repeated every time I came home from a long three week run. Obviously my wife was glad to see me too, but I won't go into what she did to me.

The new truckers have it a lot easier than their wives. They are distracted with all the new things they are learning; the excitement of actually driving an 18 wheeler; seeing new parts of the country from a perspective that you just don't get from a passenger car; meeting and talking with other new truckers and old truckers; walking around truck stops and seeing all the things they offer; learning how to set up their sleeping berths, and on and on. New drivers simply have very limited time to feel sorry for themselves or to think of anything else except driving safe, and completing all the tasks that are required of them each and every day. The only time they actually have to relax is at the end of their day while they are curled up in their bunk in the back of the truck. But even then, they are so exhausted with the newness of everything; they usually go right to sleep, after calling the wife of course.

All the break-in companies will allow you to bring your wife with you after about 6 months of accident free driving. Once you can demonstrate you can drive safely and responsibly, you can bring you wife and older children (age varies with each company) with you. As I had mentioned previously, all of the wives I spoke with who were traveling with their husbands, really enjoyed it.

Just before I published this book, I had a great phone conversation with John White, editor and publisher of Pro-Trucker Magazine (www.Pro-TruckerMagazine.com) about the poem, 'The Big Rig', by Dave Madill, that I included in the front of this book. Dave Madill also published several books on trucking. John White was kind enough to pass on some information on a great web site for wives of truckers, www.atruckerswife.com. This website helps support wives of truckers and gives them a variety of valuable resources.

One of the events this organization helps organize is a trucker's wife convention. From viewing the photos from this event, posted on their web site, it looks like a lot of fun. I was pleased to see my old employer, Schneider National, is a gold sponsor of this event.

Another good site I found on www.atruckerswife.com, was a site that helps support women in the trucking industry. The site, www.WomenInTrucking.org, was established to encourage the employment of women in the trucking industry. Their site has a wealth of good information related to women in the trucking industry.

It was good to see that there is a site like this, just for women. There were a few women in my training class and for the most part, they all did just as well as the men and on occasion, they outperformed some of the men.

I only saw a few women truck drivers on the road, and most of them appeared to be driving with who I assumed was their husbands. I remember helping this one new female trucker, who, while trying to drop a full trailer, was struggling with the rear tandems on her trailer. The tandem release handle used to retract the pins from the rail that the rear tandems slide on, would not stay in place. So the pins would keep popping back into the holes in the rail, preventing her from sliding her tandems. I shared with her a little trick I learned earlier for this type of situation. I showed her how to use a pair of locking vice grips to clamp down on the handle, next to the rail, keeping the pins retracted so she could slide the tandems. Then simply remove the vice grips, and the pins pop back into their holes, securing the rear tandem wheels. I always loved helping other drivers whenever I could. It just feels good to help people.

There is certainly no reason women cannot do this job as well as men. The only exception I can think of is in the case of the flatbed truck. From what I observed, those driving flatbed's often had to be really strong and tough while tying down and securing the huge variety of loads they have to deal with as well as handling those really heavy tarps to cover those loads that were required to be covered. But I am sure there are some female flatbed drivers out there.

CHAPTER 26

DEPARTMENT OF TRANSPORTATION MEDICAL REQUIREMENTS

In order to be physically qualified to operate a commercial vehicle you have to obtain a medical examiner's certificate stating that you are physically qualified to operate a commercial vehicle. Before making any commitments to any school or trucking company, make an appointment with your doctor. Tell them you need a physical for a commercial driver's license. You don't want to go through all the training and ground work just to find out you can't pass the physical.

The Department of Transportation standards are getting tougher. They are beginning to set standards much higher than they were in the past. The result is that many current drivers, when they go back to get their new Medical Examiner's Certificate (every 2 years), they find they no longer meet the standards. If they are good employees, some trucking companies can often find them none driving positions, but there are never any guarantees.

All commercial motor vehicle drivers driving intrastate commerce (In State only/ not crossing State Lines) are subject to the physical qualification regulations of their states. All 50 states have adapted their regulations based on some of the federal requirements. Many states grant waivers for certain medical conditions. Visit www.aamva.org/cdl-program, (American Association of Motor Vehicle Administrators) for more specifics and state by state medical certification requirements.

All commercial motor vehicle drivers driving interstate commerce within the U.S. (across state lines) must obtain medical certification from a medical examiner.

In addition, pursuant to 49CFR391.42 (www.fmcsa.dot.gov) (Federal Motor Carrier Safety Administration) you must have all of the following:

1. Have all limbs (including foot, leg, hand and arm) or have been granted a waiver.
2. Have no impairment of hand or finger, which keeps you from performing pinching and power gripping activities.

3. Have no impairment of the arm or leg which keeps you from performing duties normally associated with operating a truck or any other injury or limitation which keeps you from performing those duties or have been granted a waiver.
4. Have no medical history or diagnosis of insulin dependent diabetes.
5. Have no current clinical diagnosis of heart disease, or any other cardiovascular disease known to cause dizziness, lightheadedness, or heart attack.
6. Have no current diagnosis of respiratory problems with lungs, breathing, asthma, etc., that may interfere with your ability to control and operate your truck.
7. Have no current diagnosis of high blood pressure, which is likely to interfere with the ability to control or operate your truck.
8. Have no history or current diagnosis of severe arthritis, muscle or joint injuries, nerve problems, or circulation problems that would interfere with the ability to control or operate your truck.
9. Have no history of or diagnosis of epilepsy or any condition, which may cause you to lose consciousness or lose the ability to safely operate and keep control of your truck.
10. Have no mental, nervous, or psychiatric disorder which may keep you from being able to safely control and operate your truck.
11. Have 20/40 vision or better with glasses/contacts. Have a distant vision of 20/40 in both eyes.
12. Be able to recognize colors of traffic signals and devices showing standard red, green, and yellow.
13. Understand a forced whisper voice in the better ear not less than 5 feet away with or without a hearing aid. If tested by a device, must not have an average hearing loss in the better ear of more than 40 decibels at 500 Hz, 1,000 Hz, and 2,000 Hz with or without a hearing aid.
14. Not use a Schedule 1 drug, amphetamine, narcotic or any other addictive medication unless it is prescribed by a medical professional that knows the driver and is familiar with the driver's history and assigned work duties, and who knows that the prescribed medication will not affect the driver's ability to safely operate a truck.

Note: A driver taking Medical Marijuana cannot be certified regardless of any doctor's prescription. In addition any state law making marijuana legal for recreational purposes has no effect on the fact that under Federal Law marijuana is still listed as a schedule 1 drug, and use of marijuana under any circumstances would bar you from obtaining Medical Certification.

15. Have no current diagnosis of alcoholism.

In addition, be aware that Section 49 CFR Section 390.3(d), gives employers the right to adopt **stricter** medical standards.

When you receive your Medical Certification, you must carry your Medical card with you whenever you are driving a commercial vehicle. In 2007 alone, as a result of roadside inspections, more than 145,000 citations were issued to drivers who did not possess their Medical Certificates and more than 42,000 citations to drivers with expired Medical Certificates.

More recently, in 2012, there were 144,126 violations involving the Medical Certification Card, such as failure to have it in your possession, expired cards, driving while unqualified, etc.

In addition, there are some basic driver qualifications and regulations that are part of the Federal Motor Carrier Regulations (FMCR) Part 391. I will review a few of the major requirements/regulations.

1. You have to be at least 21 years of age
2. You have to be able to read and speak English well enough to understand highway traffic signs and to respond to officials who may ask you questions. You also need to be able to talk with the general public and be understood. Obviously if your English skills are too poor, you will not meet this standard.
3. If you have some sort of disability or severe injury, you may still be able to drive a commercial vehicle. It is possible to be granted an exception and obtain a Skill Performance Evaluation Certificate from FMCSA. Check with Department of Transportation for more information.
4. You have to demonstrate that you know how to secure a load in your trailer or on your flatbed trailer. There are various ways to secure a load using loading straps, air bags, friction mats, etc., all of which you will learn about when you go through the company training. This is important because if the cargo you are carrying shifts or falls, it could cause your trailer to roll. Drivers have also been injured while opening the back of a trailer and having the cargo tumble out on top of them. There are some paper companies that are very serious about this danger and

require all drivers who are delivering heavy paper products to their facility, like bales of cardboard or huge rolls of paper, to use safety straps on their trailer doors, as well as wear a safety helmet and safety glasses. These safety straps prevent the doors from flying open if there has been a shift in the cargo and it is leaning against the trailer doors. Even though this is a serious safety issue, it is not one I had to deal with that much. I was only required to secure one load consisting of cases of beer that had been pre-loaded into the trailer, but not sealed. For whatever reason, this particular company leaves it up to the drivers to secure the load. So I put two loading straps across the last row of product to keep it from falling over. Other than that, every trailer I had live loaded was secured by the warehouse personnel with air bags and shrink wrap. All the other trailers I hooked up had been pre-loaded and sealed, so I was not able to inspect the contents. Most of these big warehouse companies know what they are doing and do a good job securing all their loads.

5. The company that you end up working for is obligated to review your driving record every year. This helps the company identify any drivers who may not be the good little drivers they claim to be. Most companies require their drivers to self report any citations of any kind, within 10 days of the incident. This means citations received in your own private vehicle as well. Your entire driving record is at issue here. If you speed and are reckless in your private vehicle, that behavior will carry over to your driving a commercial truck as well. In addition every year all commercial drivers are required to submit a document called a 'Violation and Review Record', even if there are no violations to report.

6. If you, as a commercial truck driver, ever receive any notice that your license has been or will be suspended or revoked, you shall notify your company before the end of the business day following the day you receive the notice. In other words, immediately!

7. If you are ever convicted of driving under the influence of alcohol or drugs, or leave the scene of an accident, you are in big trouble. You can kiss your commercial drivers license good bye.

8. You cannot drive a commercial vehicle unless you have been certified by a doctor every 2 years.

9. Some medical conditions like diabetes mellitus, high blood pressure, epilepsy, etc., can cause you to lose consciousness and thereby your ability to control a motor vehicle. So for your safety

as well the safety of other drivers and the public in general, you will not be permitted to drive a commercial vehicle. This regulation is a result of numerous lives being lost due to truck drivers who have became suddenly ill or lost consciousness due to their medical conditions. This is a no-brainer. If you have these conditions, you will need to find another occupation.

10. Now, in reference to the above, if you disagree and feel your condition will not impact the safety of the public as well as yourself, you can apply for a resolution of conflict of a medical evaluation. In this appeal you must include the drivers name and address, what company you work for and the names of all the doctors involved in your case. Contact DOT for details.

11. You have to have visual acuity of at least 20/40 in each eye, with or without corrective lenses. In addition you need to have a field of vision of at least 70 degrees and be able to recognize the colors of traffic signals and any devices showing the standard red, green and amber.

12. You must be medically examined and determined to be physically qualified every 2 years. If you subsequently develop some disqualifying injury or illness after obtaining your Medical Qualification Certificate, you need to be recertified by a doctor before you can return to driving a commercial vehicle.

If you currently hold a Commercial Drivers License, be aware that a driver is disqualified from operating a commercial vehicle for the following offenses:

Conviction or forfeiture of bond for the following criminal offenses while driving a commercial motor vehicle (CMV):

1. Driving a CMV while under the influence of alcohol.
2. Driving a CMV while under the influence of a disqualifying drug or other controlled substances.
3. Transporting or possessing a disqualifying drug or controlled substance.
4. Leaving the scene of an accident that involves a CMV.
5. Using a CMV to commit a felony.
6. Using a CMV to violate an *Out-of-Service order.*

CHAPTER 27

FEDERAL MOTOR CARRIER SAFETY ADMINISTRATION (FMCSA), COMPLIANCE, SAFETY, ACCOUNTABILITY (CSA) AND THE BEHAVIOR ANALYSIS AND SAFETY IMPROVEMENT CATEGORIES (BASIC'S)

One of the new enforcement tools implemented by the Department of Transportation (DOT), Federal Motor Carrier Safety Administration (FMCSA) is the Safety Measurement System (SMS), the Compliance, Safety and Accountability (CSA), and the Behavior Analysis and Safety Improvement Categories (BASIC's). It is very important that you have a working knowledge of these new enforcement tools so you will understand the scores that result from the information gathered by roadside inspections.

Within the Compliance, Safety and Accountability (CSA) Operation Model, the Safety, Measurement System (SMS) qualifies the on-road safety performance of carriers and drivers to identify candidates for interventions, determine the specific problems that the carrier or driver exhibits, and to monitor whether safety problems are improving or worsening.

SMS uses motor carriers data from roadside inspections, including all safety-based violations, State reported crashes, and the Federal Motor Carrier census to qualify performance in the Behavior Analysis and Safety Improvement Categories (BASIC), which are listed and described later in this chapter.

This new enforcement model assigns a point/percentage value to various violations. The more critical/serious the violation or incident the more weight/points/percentage it is given.

All violations are taken into account. Everything from moving violations to violations found during a roadside inspections. Carriers are also scored based on this same information. So when you are pulled into a roadside inspection or weight station, the BASIC (Behavior Analysis and Safety Improvement Categories), information/scores, which I will explain below, are sent to roadside inspectors as a tool in the decision of whether to inspect and what level to inspect a specific truck and trailer.

In other words, as you approach a weigh station/road side inspection station, the transponder on your windshield sends them information on your truck and your company. If you work for a company that has a good reputation and has a very low CSA score, they will probably send your transponder the green signal, which allow you to by-pass the weight station or inspection. But if your company has been involved in numerous violations and has a high CSA score, they will pull you in and probably conduct a detailed inspection. This is a very simplified explanation, but I think you get my drift. When I worked for Schneider National, I rarely got pulled into a weigh station, and those few times I did, I never got pulled into an inspection after the initial drive-thru weigh-in, with the exception of the missing Haz-Mat placard mentioned in a previous chapter.

This is why I stressed at the very beginning of this book, to be careful which company you decide to go to work for. You simply do not need the extra grief of working for a bad carrier. So do your homework and avoid working for marginal carriers.

Company Snapshot

There is a DOT web site you can go to in order to get some information on a specific trucking company. Go to: http://safer.fmcsa.dot.gov/companysnapshot.aspx. According to the DOT website, this company snapshot is a concise electronic record of a company's identification, size, commodity information, and safety record, including the safety rating (if any), a roadside out of service inspection summary, and crash information.

The company snapshot is available via an ad-hoc query, FREE of charge. After visiting the site and conducting searches by name only, I found that searching by the known name of the company is not the most efficient method of searching. I was surprised at the large number of companies with similar names as the one I was searching for. Often the name I inserted into the query box was in fact not the 'legal' name of the company. So, I recommend obtaining the USDOT number of the company you are researching and conducting your search that way in order to save time wadding through all the companies that have similar names. Just call the company and they will be glad to give you their USDOT number.

CSA Measurement System

Now, I apologize, but I must go into some of the <u>very dry details</u> of the Compliance, Safety, and Accountability (CSA) that the Federal Motor Carrier Safety Administration (FMCSA) has put into place. These new enforcement tools are something you <u>really need to understand</u> and how they affect your ability to continue working as a truck driver.

There has been a lot of press on this topic and a lot of angry truck drivers complaining about unequal enforcement and application of the new rules. These rules are new and currently under review, so changes may be coming soon. Here are the basics.

CSA Measurement System—The CSA measurement system was developed to help reduce commercial vehicle (CMV) crashes, fatalities, and injuries on the nation's highways. The CSA measurement system evaluates safety of carriers and CMV drivers based on unsafe behaviors that lead to crashes, as follows:

1. It calculates safety performance based on seven Behavior Analysis and Safety Improvement Categories (BASICS), which I cover below.
2. It weights time and severity of violations based on relation to crash risk.
3. It uses crash records and All safety-based violations found at roadside.
4. It measures carrier safety performance.
5. It includes a new tool for use by Safety Investigators to assess driver safety performance.
6. In the near future, measurement results will support <u>future Safety Fitness Determinations</u>.

(Please re-read #6, "Future Safety Fitness Determinations". If I have to spell out what that means, your already in trouble. Remember what I said about tougher physical standards in the future .... well here it is in black and white!)

Behavior Analysis and Safety Improvement Categories (BASIC's)

1. **Unsafe Driving**—Operation of a commercial motor vehicle (CMV) by drivers in a dangerous or careless manner. Examples: Speeding, reckless driving, improper lane change, and inattention. (FMCSR Parts 392 and 397)

2. **Fatigued Driving/Hours of Service (HOS)**—Operation of CMV by drivers who are ill, fatigued or in noncompliance with the Hours of Service (HOS) regulations. This BASIC includes violations of regulations pertaining to logbooks as they relate to HOS requirements and the management of CMV driver fatigue. Examples: HOS, logbook, and operating a CMV while ill or fatigued. (FMCSR Parts 392 and 397)

3. **Driver Fitness**—Operation of CMV by drivers who are unfit to operate a CMV due to lack of training, experience, or medical qualifications. Examples: Failure to have a valid and appropriate commercial driver's license and being medically unqualified to operate a CMV. (FMCSR Parts 383 and 391)

4. **Controlled Substance/Alcohol**—Operation of CMV by drivers who are impaired due to alcohol, illegal drugs, and misuse of prescription or over the counter medications. Examples: Use or possession of controlled substances/alcohol. (FMCSR Parts 382 and 392)

5. **Vehicle Maintenance**—Failure to properly maintain a CMV. Examples: Brakes, lights and other mechanical defects and failure to make required repairs. (FMCSR Parts 393 and 396)

6. **Hazardous Material (HM) Compliance**—Unsafe handling of HM on a CMV. Example violations: Release of HM from package, no shipping papers (carrier), and no placards/markings when required. (FMCSR Part 397 and Hazardous Materials Regulations Parts 171, 172, 173, 177, 178, 179 and 180).

7. **Crash Indicator**—Histories or patterns of high crash involvement, including frequency and severity. It is based on information from State reported crashes.

A carrier's measurement for each of the BASIC categories listed above depends on:

1. The number of adverse safety events (violations related to that BASIC category or crashes).
2. The severity of violations or crashes.
3. When the adverse safety events occurred (more recent events are weighted more heavily).

After a measurement is determined, the carrier is then placed in a safety event group of carriers (e.g., other carriers with similar numbers of inspections). Percentiles from 0 to 100 are then determined by comparing the BASIC measurements of the carrier to the measurements of other carriers in the safety event group. 100 indicates the worst performance.

You can improve your percentile rank in the Safety Measurement System (SMS), Behavior Analysis and Safety Improvement Categories (BASIC'S) by receiving new inspections that are free of violations.

Note: As it stands now, ANY accident involving commercial driver, whether the truck driver was at fault or NOT, adds points to a carrier's and drivers score. The trucking industry is trying to get that changed so the scores are reflective of a driver's TRUE danger to the public.

Interventions—If one or more of a carriers BASIC percentiles exceed a threshold, the carrier then becomes a candidate for an 'intervention'. Typically, the intervention process starts with a warning letter, which provides the carrier with an opportunity to review its performance and make improvements without further FMCSA involvement. Thresholds vary depending on the type of carrier and the BASIC score. For example, since the consequences of passenger or hazardous material crashes are typically more severe, lower Intervention Thresholds are in place for these types of carriers.

New Mandatory GPS Navigation Training

In connection with what I said earlier in this book about getting lost and using GPS navigation systems, FMCSA will be making GPS training mandatory when it issues its 'Entry-level Commercial Drivers License Operator Rule', sometime in late 2013.

This new Rule was requested after a New York study showed a big increase in low bridge accidents caused by using inappropriate GPS systems that don't show low bridges, hazmat routes or other information relevant to truckers.

These poor GPS systems were responsible for <u>more than 80%</u> of these low bridge impacts/accidents.

DOT Dangers of Texting Videos

While doing research for this book I also came across a web site run by the U.S. Department of Transportation, that really had an impact on me, and so I am going to share that site with you, in hopes that you watch all the short 3 minute videos. There are about 12 videos, and they are well worth watching. I also hope you will encourage your children who drive to view these videos. Personally I think every high school should take an hour to show all these videos. They are that powerful. You can access the information in one of two ways: <u>www.distraction.gov</u>, then click on the tab at the top labeled 'Faces'. You can also go to <u>www.youtube.com</u>, and then type in the search bar, 'Faces of Distraction'.

CHAPTER 28

NORTH AMERICAN STANDARD DRIVER/ VEHICLE INSPECTION LEVELS

The Information in the next 4 chapters comes directly from the Federal Motor Carrier Safety Administration web site: http://fmcsa.dot.gov., type 'road side inspections' in search bar. After reviewing the FMCSA web site I simply could not find the information I wanted to include in this book. I spoke with a FMCSA employee, Steve Kleszezynshi, who was very helpful and sent me the link above.

When I started driving I had no idea what to expect if I was ever pulled into a full inspection. I want you to at least have some idea of what is involved. In this chapter I want to edify you on the various levels of inspection that can take place when you are pulled into a weight station, inspection station or just about anywhere. So when you hear about these various levels you will have a better idea of what is involved.

Level I
North American Standard Inspection

An inspection that includes examination of driver's license, medical examiner's certificate and waiver, if applicable, alcohol and drugs, driver's record of duty status as required, hours of service, seat belt. Vehicle inspection report, brake system, coupling devices, exhaust system, frame, fuel system, turn signals, brake lamps, tail lamps, head lamps, lamps on projecting loads, safe loading, steering mechanism, suspension, tires, van and open-top trailer bodies, wheels and rims, windshield wipers, emergency exits on buses and Hazardous Material requirements, as applicable.

Level II
Walk-Around Driver/Vehicle Inspection

An examination that includes each of the items specified under the North American Standard Inspection. As a minimum, Level II inspections must include examination of: driver's license, medical certificate and waiver, alcohol and drugs, driver's record of duty status as required, hours of service, seat belt, vehicle inspection report, brake system, coupling devices, exhaust system, frame, fuel system, turn signals, brake lamps, tail lamps, head lamps, lamps on projecting loads, safe loading, steering mechanism, suspension, tires, van and open-top trailer bodies, wheels and rims, windshield wipers, emergency exits on buses, and Hazardous Material requirements, as applicable. It is contemplated that the walk-around driver/vehicle inspection will include only those items which can be inspected without physically getting under the vehicle.

Level III
Driver-Only Inspection

A roadside examination of the driver's license, medical certification and waiver, if applicable, driver's record of duty status as required, hours of service, seat belt, vehicle inspection report, and Hazardous Material requirements, as applicable.

Level IV
Special Inspections

Inspections under this heading typically include a one-time examination of a particular item. These examinations are normally made in support of a study or to verify or refute a suspected trend.

Level V
Vehicle-Only Inspection

An inspection that includes each of the vehicle inspection items specified under the North American Inspection (Level I), without a driver present, conducted at any location.

Level VI
Enhanced NAS Inspection for Radioactive Shipments

An inspection for select radiological shipments, which include inspection procedures, enhancements to the Level I inspection, radiological requirements, and enhanced out-of-service criteria. Select radiological shipments include only highway route controlled as defined by title 49 section 173.403 and all transuranics.

CHAPTER 29

THE SAFETY MEASUREMENT SYSTEM (SMS) SEVERITY TABLES

Below is a sample of severity points for some typical roadside violations. The severity points for all violations can be found at: http://csa.fmcsa. dot.gov/yourrole/drivers.aspx, in Appendix A of the SMS Methodology.

The severity weights reflect the relative importance of each violation within each particular Behavior Analysis and Safety Improvement Category (BASIC). They cannot be compared meaningfully across the various BASICs. For example, a violation with a severity weight of 7 in the Vehicle Maintenance BASIC is not intended to be equivalent to a violation with a severity weight of 7 in the Driver Fitness BASIC. The violation severity weights are currently being reviewed based on feedback from stakeholders.

Violation Description Shown on Roadside Inspection Severity Weight

392.2C Failure to obey traffic control device. 6
392.2DH Headlamps—Failure to dim when required. 3
392.2FC Following to close. 5
392.2LC Improper lane change. 5
392.2LV Lane restriction violation. 3
392.2P Improper passing. 5
392.2PK Unlawful parking and/or leaving vehicle in the roadway. 1
392.2R Reckless driving. 10
392.2RR Railroad grade crossing violation. 5
392.2S Speeding 1-5 mph over limit. 1
392.2SLLS2 State/Local Laws—Speeding 6-10 mph over limit. 4
392.2SLLS3 State/Local Laws—Speeding 11-14 mph over limit. 7
392.2SLLS4 State/Local Laws—Speeding 16 or more mph over limit. 10

392.2SLLSWZ State/Local Laws—Speeding in a work/construction zone. 10

392.2SLLT State/Local Laws—Operating a CMV while texting. 10

392.2T Improper turns. 5

392.2Y Failure to yield right-of-way. 5

392.2H Hours-of-Service (HOS) Violation. 7

392.2WC Wheel (mud) flaps missing or defective. 1

CHAPTER 30

ROADSIDE INSPECTION
ACTIVITY SUMMARY

From the same FMCSA website cited above, below are statistics from roadside inspections conducted in the United States (Canada and Mexico excluded) for the years 2009 through 2012. I am including these only because I personally had always wondered just how active are the local, state and federal authorities in conducting inspections and finding violations. By the way, in the graph below, when a driver or vehicle is put out of service as a result of the inspection, they are shut down until the violations are addressed. The short symbol for 'Out of Service' is OOS.

Activity Summary	CY 2009			CY 2010			CY 2011			CY 2012			Total
	Fed	State	Total	Fed	State	Total	Fed	State	Total	Fed	State	Total	
Number of Inspections	42,489	3,175,816	3,218,305	37,574	3,194,884	3,232,458	37,503	3,203,130	3,240,633	35,442	3,152,670	3,188,112	
With No Violations	20,330	1,086617	1,106,947	16,240	1,147,713	1,163,953	17,995	1,244,934	1,262,929	17,939	1,274,089	1,292,028	
With Violations	22,159	2,089,199	2,111,358	21,334	2,047,171	2,068,505	19,508	1,958,196	1,977,704	17,503	1,878,581	1,896,084	
With OOS Violations	6,229	609,452	615,681	5,663	576,457	582,120	5,342	582,010	587,352	4,688	570,744	575,432	
Number of Violations	61,414	6,312,617	6,374,031	59,932	6,296,835	6,356,767	54,010	5,860,673	5,914,683	47,113	5,461,997	5,509,110	
OOS Violations	8,697	977,517	986,214	7,790	915,665	923,455	7,318	920,074	927,392	6,302	895,774	902,076	
Other Violations	52,717	5,335,100	5,387,817	52,142	5,381,170	5,433,312	46,692	4,940,599	4,987,291	40,811	4,566,223	4,607,034	

*Data Source: FMCSA Motor Carrier Management Information System (MCMIS).

CHAPTER 31

ROADSIDE INSPECTIONS, DRIVER VIOLATIONS

In the next 3 chapters, I am going to cover material that I wish I had known when I started. As I was going through training, and then later driving on my own, I often wondered, exactly what type of violations are these inspectors at weigh stations are looking for. Besides the standard things I learned in my training, I was curious about the specific violations and how often those violations were found during a roadside inspection. The table below reflects violations by CMV drivers for 2012.

I gleaned this information from the FMCSA/DOT web sites as noted above in previous chapter.

	Roadside Inspections for 2012—Driver Violations Description	# of Violations					
1	Log Violation (General /Form And Manner).	157,742			2	Driver Record of Duty Status Not Current.	108,381
3	Driver Not in Possession of Medical Certificate.	92,006			4	Speeding 6-10 MPH Over Limit.	55,996
5	Failure to Use Seat Belt While Operating CMV.	53,329			6	Requiring or Permitting Driver to Drive After 14 Hours On Duty.	45,127
7	Failure to Obey Traffic Control Device.	37,274			8	False Report of Drivers Record of Duty Status.	36,547
9	Expired Medical Examiners Certificate.	31,931			10	No Driver Record of Duty Status	30,624

11	Speeding 1-5 MPH Over Limit.	27,382				12	Driver Failure to Retain Previous 7 day's logs.	26,330
13	Requiring or Permitting Driver to Drive More Than 11 Hours.	25,102				14	Speeding 11-14 MPH Over Limit.	22,562
15	Operating a Property Carrying Vehicle Without Possessing a Valid Medical Certificate.	14,879				16	Operating a CMV Without a CDL.	14,632
17	Speeding 15 or More Over Limit.	13,645				18	Driving Beyond 14 Hour Duty Period (Property Carrying Vehicle).	13,623
19	Driver Lacking Valid License For Type of Vehicle Being Operated.	13,573				20	Lane Restriction Violation	10,116
21	Following Too Close.	9,705				22	Improper Lane Change.	9,079
23	Driving Beyond 11 Hour Limit in 14 Hour Period (Property Carrying Vehicle).	7,299				24	Using a Hand Held Mobile Phone While Operating a CMV.	7,267
25	Speeding in Work/ Construction Zone.	6,176				26	Driver Lacking Physical Qualifications.	6,130
27	Hours of Service (HOS).	6,130				28	Non-English Speaking Driver.	5,141
29	Driving a CMV While Disqualified.	4,579				30	60/70 Hour rule Violation.	4,124
31	Unlawful Parking and/or Leaving Vehicle In The Roadway.	3,948				32	Improper Passing.	3,507
33	Improper Medical Examiners Certificate Form.	3,327				34	Unauthorized Passenger On Board CMV.	3,232
35	Speeding.	3,127				36	Using or Equipping a CMV With Radar Detector.	2,949
37	Possession/Use/ Under The Influence of Alcohol-4 Hours Prior To Duty.	2,670				38	Driving a CMV While Disqualified.	2,461

39	On-Board Recording Device Information Not Available.	2,288				40	Unqualified Driver.	2,169
41	Failure to Yield Right of Way.	2,043				42	Driver Disqualified From Operating CMV.	1,830
43	Improper Turns.	1,608				44	Failure To Use Hazard Warning Flashers.	1,585
45	Operating a CMV With Improper CDL Group.	1,425				46	Driving A CMV while disqualified. Suspended for safety related or unknown reason and in the state of drivers license issuance.	1,397
47	Driver Uses or In Possession of Drugs.	1,265				48	New Truck Req./ Perm. Property CMV Driver to Drive After 70 Hours On Duty in 8 Days.	1,221
49	Driver does not have a valid operator's license for the CMV being operated.	1,215				50	No Valid Medical Waiver in Driver's Possession.	1,199
51	Driving a CMV while CDL is suspended for a safety-related or unknown reason and in the state of the driver's license issuance.	1,055				52	Interstate Drive Under 21 Years of Age.	936
53	Operating a CMV while ill/fatigued.	881				54	Operating a Property-Carrying Vehicle Without Possessing a Valid Medical Certificate. Previously Cited On (Date).	779

55	Reckless Driving	761				56	Onboard Recording Device Information Requirements Not Met.	730
57	Driving a CMV While CDL is Suspended For Non-Safety Related Reason and In State of Driver's License Issuance.	631				58	Driver Operating a CMV Without Proper Endorsements or In Violation of Restrictions.	626
59	Driving a CMV While Disqualified. Suspended for Non-Safety Related Reason And In The State of Driver's Issuance.	590				60	Driving After Being Declared Out-Of-Service.	485
61	State/Local Ordinances Regulations.	476				62	Operating a Passenger-Carrying Vehicle Without Possessing a Valid Medical Certificate.	437
63	Onboard Recording Device Improper Form and Manner.	417				66	No Tank Vehicle Endorsement on CDL.	396
67	No Hazardous Material Endorsement On CDL.	378				68	Driving a CMV while disqualified. Suspended for a non-safety-related reason and outside the state of driver's license issuance.	375
69	Driving a CMV While Texting.	366				70	Driving a CMV While CDL is Suspended For a Non-Safety Related Reason And Outside the State of Driver's License Issuance.	348
71	Operating On a Learner's Permit Without Valid Driver's License.	345				72	Smoking Within 25 Feet of a HM Vehicle.	274

73	Driving a CMV While Disqualified. Suspended For Safety Related or Unknown Reason And Outside The Drivers License State of Issuance.	260				74	Violating Airbrake Restriction	255
75	Onboard Recording Device Failure and Driver Failure to Reconstruct Duty Status.	244				76	Driving a CMV While Disqualified. Suspended For Non-Safety Related Reason and Outside The State of Drivers License issuance.	243
77	Driver Must Be Able To Understand Highway Traffic Signs and Signals In The English language.	233				78	Headlamp—Failure to Dim When Required.	223
79	Operating a CMV While Texting.	222				80	Operating a CMV On a Learners Permit Without a CDL Holder In Vehicle.	180
81	State/Local Laws – Operating a CMV While Texting.	174				82	Failure to Stop At Railroad Crossing – Placard.	171
83	Fatigue – Operating a Property-Carrying CMV While Impaired By Fatigue.	162				84	Driver Training Requirements.	158
85	Failure To Stop At Railroad Crossing— HM Cargo.	143				86	Onboard Recording Device Does Not Display Required Information.	141
87	Violating OOS Order Pursuant to 392.5(A)/(B).	141				88	Requiring Driver To Use A Hand-Held Mobile Tel. While Operating a CMV.	138
89	Operating a CMV With More Than One Driver's License.	130				90	10 – Hour Rule Violation (Passenger CMV).	123

91	Failure To Use Caution For Hazardous Condition.	123				92	Operating on Learner's Permit Without CDL Holder.	120
93	Railroad Grade Crossing Violation.	108				94	Schedule Run To Necessitate Speeding.	103
95	Illness – Operating a CMV while impaired by illness or other cause.	93				96	No Double/Triple Trailer Endorsement on CDL.	88
97	No Passenger Vehicle Endorsement on CDL.	81				98	Driving After 10 Hour Driving Limit (Passenger Carrying Vehicle).	72
99	15, 20, 70/80 HOS Violations (Alaska-Property).	71				100	Failure To Stop At Railroad Crossing – Bus.	69
101	Driving After 70 Hours On Duty In a 8 Day Period (Passenger Carrying Vehicle).	66				102	Driving After 15 Hours On Duty (Passenger Carrying Vehicle).	46
103	16 Hour Rule Violation (Property).	43				104	Violation of HOS Regulations—Migrant Workers.	26
105	Driving After 60 Hours On Duty in a 7 Day Period (Property)	24				106	Unsafe Bus Operations.	23
107	34 Hour Restart Violation (Property).	19				108	No School Bus Endorsement on CDL.	15
109	Fatigue—Operating a Passenger Carrying CMV While Impaired By Fatigue.	11				110	Failure To Comply With Imminent Hazard OOS Order.	9
111	Bus—Standees Forward Of The Standee Line.	8				112	No Doctor's Certificate In Possession.	8
113	Failure To Comply With 392.82—Using Mobile Phone While Operating a CMV—HM.	7				114	Adverse Driving Conditions Violations. (Alaska)	6

115	Driving of Vehicle—Migrant Workers.	6				116	Driving After 60 Hours On Duty In a 7 Day Period (Passenger Carrying Vehicle).	5
117	Failure To Stop At Railroad Crossing—Chlorine.	5				118	Driver Not Physically Qualified.	4
119	Operating a CMV With More Than One Driver's License.	4				120	Unnecessary Delay In HM Transportation to Destination.	4

*Total number of Driver Inspections in 2012: 3,074,069
*Total number of Driver Violations in 2012: 957,545
*Total number of Out Of Service (OOS) Violations in 2012: 190,275

CHAPTER 32

ROADSIDE INSPECTIONS, VEHICLE VIOLATIONS

	Roadside Inspections for 2012—Driver Violations Description	# of Violations						
1	Operating Vehicle Not Having The Required Lamps.	428,805				2	No/Defective Lighting Devices/ Reflective Devices/ Projected.	200,249
3	Tire—Other Tread Depth Less Than 2/32 of Inch.	181,822				4	Clamp/Roto-Chamber Type Brakes Out of Adjustment.	174,503
5	Inspection/Repair and Maintenance Parts And Accessories.	172,913				6	Operating a CMV Without Periodic Inspection.	159,143
7	No/Discharged/ Unsecured Fire Extinguisher.	146,306				8	Oil and/or Grease Leak.	103,494
9	Failing To Secure Brake Hose/Tubing Against Mechanical Damage.	100,324				10	Inoperative Turn Signal.	88,223
11	Stop Lamp Violation.	84,237				12	Automatic Brake Adjuster CMV Manufactured on/or After 10/20/1994.	83,941
13	Inoperative/Defective Brake.	78,969				14	No/Insufficient Warning Devices.	64,582
15	Windshield Wipers Inoperative/Defective.	62,712				16	Damaged or Discolored Windshield.	52,920
17	Brake Tubing And Hose Adequacy.	50,381				18	Inoperative Head Lamps	48,865
19	Brakes (General)	46,339				20	Inoperative Tail Lamp	45,810
21	Brake Connections With Leaks/ Constrictions.	41,440				22	Flat Tire or Fabric Exposed.	37,774

23	Tire—Flat and/or Audible Leak.	30,203				24	No/Improper Breakaway or Emergency Brake.	29,862
25	Tire—Ply or Belt Material Exposed.	29,787				26	Axle Positioning Parts Defective/ Missing.	27,429
27	Exhaust Leak Under Truck Cab and/or Sleeper.	26,432				28	Inoperative/ Defective Hazard Warning Lamp.	26,080
29	Inadequate Brakes For Safe Stopping	25,122				30	Power Steering Violations.	23,037
31	Wheel Fasteners Loose and/or Missing.	22,206				32	Frame Cracked/ Loose/Sagging/ Broken.	21,137
33	ABS—Malfunctioning Lamps.	20,077				34	Steering System Components Worn/ Welded/ Missing.	18,628
35	Glazing Permits Less Than 70 Percent of Light.	18,137				36	Non-Compliance With Head Lamp Requirements.	17,686
37	No or Defective Brake Warning Device.	17,145				38	Tire Tread and/or Sidewall Separation.	16,622
39	Tire—Front Tread Depth Less Than 4/32 of Inch.	16,318				40	Horn Inoperative.	15,930
41	Truck Tractor Manufactured On Or After 7/1/1997 With No Retro Reflective Sheeting Or Reflex Reflectors On Mud Flaps.	15,848				42	Brake Out of Adjustment.	15,120
43	Brake House Or Tubing Chafing and/or Kinking Under Vehicle.	14,937				44	Failure To Prevent Cargo Shifting.	14,797
45	Insufficient Brake Linings	14,789				46	Leaf Spring Assembly Defective/ Missing	14,571
47	Wheel (Mud) Flaps Missing or Defective.	13,882				48	Failing to Secure Vehicle Equipment.	13,497
49	Tires (General)	13,248				50	No spare Fuses As Required.	12,942
51	Tire Under Inflated.	11,884				52	Damaged Securement System/ Tiedowns.	10,694

53	Air Suspension Pressure Loss.	10,692				54	Circuit/ Signal Manufactured On Or After 3/1/1997, Single Unit CMV Manufactured On Or After 3/1/1998.	10,487
55	Leaking/Spilling/ Blowing/ Falling Cargo.	10,384				56	Tire—Load Weight Rating/ Under Inflated.	10,337
57	Improper Or No Wiring Protection As Required.	10,014				58	Failing To Secure Load.	9,552
59	Failing To Inspect/Use Emergency Equipment.	9,391				60	Insufficient Tiedowns; Without Headboard/ Blocking.	9,219
61	Brake—Reserve System Pressure Loss.	9,160				62	ABS—All Other CMV's Manufactured On Or After 3/1/1998 Air Brake System.	9,130
63	No Or Defective Automatic Trailer Brake.	9,007				64	ABS –All Tractors Manufactured On Or After 3/1/1997 Air Brake System.	8,949
65	Failing To Secure Brake Hose/ Tubing Against Mechanical Damage.	8,742				66	Improper Battery Installation.	8,481
67	Failure To Correct Defects Noted On Inspection report.	8,356				68	Tire—Cut Exposing Ply and/or Belt Material.	8,181
69	Loose/ Unfastened Tiedown.	7,919				70	Wheel/ Rim Cracked Or Broken.	7,536
71	Exhaust System Location	7,503				72	Hood Not Securely Fastened.	7,037
73	No or Inadequate Driver Vehicle Inspection Report.	6,862				74	No/ Improper Heavy Vehicle/ Machine Securement.	6,102
75	Driver Failing To Conduct Pre-Trip Inspection.	5,775				76	Windshields Required.	5,399
77	ABS—Malfunctioning Indicator Connection From Towed CMV Manufactured On Or After 3/1/2001	5,124				78	Adjustable Axle Locking Pin Missing/ Disengaged.	5,076

79	Lower Rear Retroreflective Sheeting/ Reflex Reflectors Manufactured On Or After 12/1/1993.	4,856				80	Brake Adjustment Indicator CMV— Manufactured On Or After 10/20/1994— External Automatic Adjustment.	4,151
81	Frame Accessories Improperly Attached.	4,097				82	Hubs—Oil and/or Grease Leaking from Hub—Inner Wheel.	3,906
83	No Means to Ensure Operable Check Valve.	3,770				84	Fuel Tank Requirement Violations.	3,759
85	Brake Connections With Leaks Under Vehicle.	3,496				86	Inadequate/ Contaminated Brake Linings.	3,453
87	Windshield— Obstructed.	3,448				88	No Brakes As Required.	3,433
89	Package Not Secure In Vehicle	3,391				90	Lamp Not Steady Burning.	3,304
91	Failing/Improper Placement Of Warning Devices.	3,227				92	Cab/Body Improperly Secured To Frame.	3,126
93	No/Improper Safety Chains/Cables For Full Trailer.	3,015				94	Cab Door Missing/ Broken.	3,010
95	No/Improper Tractor Protection Valve.	2,929				96	Placard Damaged, Deteriorated, Or Obscured.	2,843
97	Warning Flag Required On Projecting Load.	2,804				98	Speedometer Inoperative/ Inadequate.	2,797
99	Must Have knowledge Of And Comply With Regulations.	2,631				100	Defective/Improper Fifth Wheel Assemblies.	2,571
101	Failure To Equip Vehicle With Two Rear Vision Mirrors.	2,530				102	Lamps Are Not Visible As Required.	2,530
103	Non-Compliant Fog/ Driving Lamps.	2,393				104	Vehicle Not Placarded As Required.	2,359
105	Cab Front bumper Missing/ Unsecured/ Protrude.	2,337				106	Exhaust System Not Securely Fastened.	2,316
107	Unsafe Operations Forbidden.	2,295				108	No Shipping Papers (Carrier).	2,268
109	Improper Exhaust Discharge (Not Rear Of Cab).	2,211				110	Fuel Tank Pipe Cap Missing.	2,106

111	Shipping Paper Accessibility.	2,079				112	Brake Connections With Leaks—Connections To Power Unit.	1,989
113	Mismatched Brake Chambers On Same Axle.	1,881				114	Emergency Response Information Missing.	1,826
115	Torsion Bar Cracked and/or Broken.	1,807				116	Cargo Not Immobilized Or Secured.	1,614
117	Inadequate Floor Condition.	1,558				118	Defective Coupling Devices For Full Trailer.	1,429
119	Mismatched Slack Adjuster Effective Length.	1,421				120	Fail To Ensure Intermodal Container Secured.	1,282
121	Defroster/Defogger Inoperative.	1,132				122	Loose Steering Column.	776

*Only 122 of 537 Vehicle Violations reflected above.
*Total number of Vehicle Inspections in 2012: 2,150,293
*Total number of Vehicle Violations in 2012: 3,526,446
*Total number of Vehicles Out-Of-Service (OOS) Violations in 2012: 629,148

CHAPTER 33

ROADSIDE INSPECTIONS, HAZARDOUS MATERIAL VIOLATIONS

	Roadside Inspections For 2012—HazMat Violations							
1	No Copy Of U.S. DOT Hazardous Materials Registration Number	3,977				2	Package Not Secure In Vehicle	3,391
3	Placard Damaged, Deteriorated Or Obscured	2,843				4	Vehicle Not Placarded As Required	2,359
5	No Shipping Papers	2,268				6	Shipping Paper Accessibility	2,079
7	Failing To Provide Carrier Required Placards	1,828				8	Emergency Response Information Required	1,826
9	Offering A HM Without Preparing A Shipping Paper (None At All)	1,256				10	No Placards/Markings When Required	1,245
11	Emergency Response (ER) Information Not Available	1,204				12	Cargo Tank Test Or Inspection Markings	1,013
13	Release of HM From Package	592				14	Failing To Enter Emergency Response Phone # On Shipping Paper	549
15	Failure To Enter Proper Shipping Name On Shipping Paper	546				16	Package/Containment Not Labeled As Required	487
17	Placard/Device Could Be Confused/ Conflict With DOT Placard	483				18	Maintenance/ Accessibility Of Emergency Response Information	477
19	State/ Local Laws Ordinances Regulations	476				20	Failing To Register With PHMSA Prior To Transporting HazMat Requiring Reg.	450

21	Failing To Enter HM Description On Shipping Paper in Manner Required	441				22	Failure To Comply With HM Regulations	427
23	Closures For Packages Must Not Be Open Or Leaking	424				24	Failing To Enter Total Qty. Of HazMat On Shipping Paper	414
25	Placard Not Reading Horizontally	399				26	Failure To Comply With Req. For HM Transportation	373
27	Wrong Or No ID Number	365				28	Form And Manner Of ER Information	354
29	Failing To Enter Packing Group On Shipping Paper	344				30	Failing To Enter ID Number On Shipping Paper	323
31	Placard Not Visible From Direction It Faces	322				32	Markings For Other Bulk Packages	316
33	Failing To Enter Basic Description Of HM In Proper Sequence	315				34	No Proper Shipping And/or ID # Marking On Non-Bulk	314
35	Placard Not Securely Affixed Or Attached	313				36	Accepting/ Transporting HM Not Prepared Properly	311
37	Manholes And Valves Not Closed Or Leak Free	302				38	Failed To Meet General Package Requirements	290
39	Failing To Enter Exemption #	278				40	Smoking Within 25 Feet Of HM Vehicle	274
41	Placard Does Not Meet Specifications	236				42	Required ID Markings Displayed	245
43	No ID Number (Portable And Cargo Tank)	235				44	Placards Not Affixed To Vehicle	228

*In the above chart I have included only the top 44 violation categories out of the 298 categories included in the full report for 2012.

*The total number of Hazmat Inspections in 2012 was: 193,174

*The total number of Hazmat violations in 2012 was : 42,732

*The total number of Hazmat Out-Of-Service (OOS) violations in 2012 was: 10,097

Data Source: FMCSA Motor Carrier management Information System (MCMIS) data snapshot as of 4/26/2013.

EPILOGUE

After 9 months of driving, I decided to call it quits. My family was planning a two month long vacation to the Philippines in December of 2012, so I chose to end my career just prior to the beginning of that vacation. No company is going to look favorably on a new driver taking a two month vacation after being on board just nine months. The Sundance Gymnastics Club also wanted me to come back to coaching, so I agreed.

What I found over nine months of driving, it is very difficult to make the kind of money that some of the trucking company ads promise. I am sure you have seen the ads indicating you can make 52k to 67k starting. Well, I don't know where those jobs are for the new driver and doubt they really exist. After six months I was making .32 cents a mile. I would stay out 3 to 4 weeks at a time and average only $500 to $600 a week.

I remember talking with a representative from Stevens Transport who told me that after 6 months with Stevens there should be no excuse for not making at least $1,000 a week. If I could find a company that would guarantee me $1,500 a week, I would consider returning to driving a truck.

Of course one way to make good money is to buy your own truck, and become an *owner operator* or *Independent Contractor*. I recommend that you first gut it out with a break in company.

Learn the ropes and make your mistakes with a break-in company. Try to think of it as paid training enabling you to learn the industry. I know the pay during those initial twelve months is not all that great, but remember, your company, not you, is taking on all the regulatory responsibilities, all the financial risks, all the administrative costs, etc. Try to keep things in perspective.

About 3 months into your new career, you can start looking into better opportunities with your existing company, or start looking at companies that are considered LTL (Less Than Truckload). Some of the benefits of working for line-haul companies are that you usually will be driving a day cab. This means no more sleeping, showering and doing you laundry at truck stops. You will either be sleeping at home and using your own shower or sleeping at a hotel that the company pays for. After you have been on the road awhile, you begin to see what a huge benefit that is.

There is always the chance that a local trucking company, headquartered in your city, may accept you as a new driver right out CDL School. I would encourage you to do some research into companies near your home that may have day time driving jobs, or very short 1 or 2 day hauls that get you home more often. You won't know unless you research local carriers.

As long as you enjoy driving, driving an 18-wheeler is a dream job. You are alone with your thoughts with no real distractions and your time is basically your own. It is the time alone that I think every person needs, and you get paid for it.

As I related in Chapter 1, after passing through the learning curve and becoming comfortable with the equipment, driving an 18-wheeler is like spending a nice relaxing day tinkering around the garage. It is very relaxing and time fly's by as you cruise down the highway.

You still have to be aware of the tremendous responsibilities and liabilities you have while driving an 18 wheeler. But once again, as long as you approach your work in a serious and professional manner, you can still enjoy the tremendous sense of freedom that this occupation offers. You just have to stick around long enough to get paid a wage you can actually live on.

As long as you commit to at least one year to learning about the industry, getting comfortable with your truck and the daily routine, I really don't think there are many jobs that offer as much variety and freedom as that of a truck driver.

The caveat is getting paid commensurate with the <u>huge</u> responsibilities and dangers that accompany this occupation. Remember, you are steering up to 80,000 lbs. (40 tons) on roads that are shared by other families. A mistake or lapse of concentration in this occupation could result in dozens of lives being lost, millions of dollars in damage and your life, if you survive, is basically never going to be the same. The law suits, just or unjust, and possible criminal charges will bury you for decades and change your life forever. This is true of any major vehicle accident, but especially true when 18-wheelers are involved.

The truck companies will offer you various other driving plans, like work one week, home one week, which is great, but you can't make a living working that kind of schedule. There are some union jobs, with companies like Safeway that pay well, but are difficult to break into unless you have lots of experience. There are also some good truck companies that will hire you at a fair wage, but only after you have a <u>minimum</u> of one year and sometimes two years experience.

Just as a side note, when I mention being away from home for 2 or 3 weeks at a time while driving an 18-wheeler, and I hear drivers complain, I can't help think that an ever increasing percentage Americans have become so lazy and unwilling to sacrifice for their family. It seems that too many Americans just seem to give up if something turns out to be harder than they thought it would be.

My wife, Meriam, is from the Philippines, and every time I go back there with her to visit, I am reminded how much they sacrifice for their families.

It is difficult to get my wife's family together during holidays because so many family members have to travel out of the country to find work. There are simply not enough jobs in the Philippines.

They are away from their spouses and children for 2 or more years, in places like Singapore, Hong Kong, Japan, Malaysia, Dubai, and other countries, trying to earn money to send to their families.

Then I think about the large number of Americans who have become so complacent and lazy, unwilling to make any sacrifices for their family. In many cases the 'family unit' no longer exists.

I believe every American should visit any one of these numerous countries where poverty is so severe, it just breaks your heart to be there, see it, and not be able to do anything about it. They will see how families work together to survive and improve the situation for the whole family.

In saying this, I am only pointing out some huge cultural differences between us and most of the rest of the world.

Once again, driving a truck really is a great job. Once you get through the initial learning curve without any major accidents or screw-ups, you will be better able to enjoy the freedom of the open road and experience a sense of relaxation you probably have never experienced before.

I hope this book helps cut the learning curve in half and puts you in a much better position to be successful in this industry.

Good luck with your search and remember to take it slow.

ABOUT THE AUTHOR

Chris was born in Denver, Colorado in 1950. He lived in Denver and the near-by suburbs of Englewood and Littleton, up until 1965. He was a freshman at Mullen High School, when his parents moved the entire family to California.

Chris did a short 6 month stay in the Sacramento area where he finished his freshman year at San Juan High School in Carmichael, California. The family then moved to Palo Alto, California, where Chris attended Palo Alto Senior High, graduating in 1969.

While attending high school, in his sophomore year, Chris participated in football and wrestling. He did fairly well in wrestling, winning a gold medal in his senior year. In his sophomore year, right after wrestling season ended, his wrestling coach (Wes Fisher) came up to Chris and 'advised' him he would be going out for the gymnastics team. Coach Wes Fisher and gymnastics coach, Ed Hart, apparently thought Chris would make a good gymnast. Chris had his reservations. Chris knew nothing about gymnastics and was not too keen on the idea. But, Chris had tremendous respect for both coaches, and followed their 'recommendation' to go out for the gymnastics team.

As it often happens in life, there are decisions we make that end up having a huge impact on the rest of our lives. Chris turned out to be a fairly good gymnast, winning over a dozen medals in his last 3 years of high school and sharing the honor of being voted 'Most Valuable Gymnast' in both his junior and senior years, along with his buddy on the team, Bill Gruber.

Gymnastics has been a part of his life ever since then. Chris has continued teaching and coaching at various gyms and colleges in his spare time. He just loves teaching.

After 3 years of attending both Foothill and DeAnza Colleges in the South Bay area of California, Chris enlisted in the U.S. Air Force in 1972. He spent almost 3 years at Grand Forks Air Force Base in Grand Forks, North Dakota. While stationed there he was a Security Policeman for the Minuteman Nuclear Missile Complex, with a short assignment in the B-52 bomber squadron. Chris also spent one year at Eielson Air Force Base near Fairbanks, Alaska. While there he worked as the alert area security supervisor for the F-4E fighter alert area.

While in the Air Force, in Grand Forks, North Dakota, Chris acted as assistant coach for the women's gymnastics team at the University of North Dakota. In addition, he was the head coach for the University's children's gymnastics program, called 'Gymnicks'. This was all conducted during his off duty time.

While stationed in Alaska, during his off duty time, Chris also taught gymnastics to the children of base personnel and attended criminology classes at the University of Alaska.

After being honorably discharged from the Air Force, Chris finished his bachelors' degree in Administration of Justice at San Jose State University, graduating in May of 1977.

In June of 1977, Chris was hired as an investigator trainee for the State of California, Department of Alcoholic Beverage Control. After 27 years as an investigator and later as a Supervising Investigator and District Supervisor, Chris retired in January of 2004.

While employed as a Supervising Investigator for the State of California, Chris also worked part time as an instructor at the South Bay Regional Police Academy in San Jose, California. Chris taught arrest and control techniques, self defense, gun take-aways, weapon retention and straight baton techniques. He also taught a class dealing with the state alcohol laws. Chris taught at the police academy for 25 years.

Prior to those 25 at the police academy, Chris began studying Aikido and taking arrest & control/ self defense and straight police baton classes from Sensei Robert Koga. While Chris was studying, practicing and teaching arrest & and control techniques under Sensei Robert Koga (KOGA Method, www.kogainst.com) he met and worked with some of the most honorable people he has ever known.

Then there is the matter of Sensei Robert Koga himself. Chris cannot say enough about this man. Sensei Koga practiced and taught martial arts the better part of 75 years. He taught the system of arrest and control that he developed (The KOGA Method) to tens of thousands of people, at hundreds of various law enforcement agencies and elite government military units, around the world and was also the author of several books on the subject.

He is a legend now, having passed away on September 8, 2013 from Mesothelioma, an asbestos related lung cancer. Sensei Koga had a tremendous impact on Chris' life and he feels very lucky to have had the opportunity to study under him all those years. Besides all the practical techniques Chris learned, more importantly, he learned how to be a good cop, how to keep his ego in check and give people the respect they deserve until they dictate otherwise, and so much more.

One of the most difficult times in Chris' life was sitting next to Sensei Koga's bed, while Sensei Koga's son, Tommy, sat on the other side of the bed holding his father's hand, watching Mr. Koga take some of his last breaths.

After retiring in 2004, Chris moved his family to Monument, Colorado, and began a new life as a full time dad.

Chris was lucky to find Sundance Studio and Gymnastics Club in Monument. He found it to be one of the best gymnastics clubs he has ever had the opportunity to coach for. The owners, Steve and Kathy Clowes, and the gym manager, Olivia Pennington, are by far some of the best coaches Chris has ever had the pleasure of teaching/coaching for, as well as some of the nicest people he has ever met.

NOTES

Chapter 11

1. -www.doctoroz.com/topic/sleep, Mehmet Oz, MD (Dr. Oz) Cardiology
    -www.sleepingpillow.org, February 22, 2011.
2. -Life Extension Magazine, Nutraceutical Uddate on Melatonin, New Reasearch Shows Impressive Health Benefits June 2007. By Debra Fulghum Bruce, PhD. www.lef.org
    -Livestrong.com, What are the Benefits of Melatonin, September 3, 2010, By Amy Pellegrini.
    -Ehow.com, Benefits of Taking Melatonin, by Sava Tang Alcantara. Livestrong.com, February 17, 2011, Benefits and Side Effects of Melatonin. By Gail Morris.
    -Smart Publications, Clarifying the Complex World of Nutrition Science. www.smart-publications.com/health-a-z/Melatonin.
    -Web MD, June 7, 2010, www.webmd.com/sleep-disorders/tc/melatonin-overview.
    -Dr. Mercola, www.mercola.com. Type in top search bar, "Melatonin Benefits", article titled 'The Many Benefits of Melatonin. Video by Russel J. Reiter, PhD, at the University of Texas.
    -Mayo Clinic, An Evidence-Based Monograph prepared by the National Standard Research Collaboration, www.mayoclinic.com/health/melatonin/nspatient-melatonin/DSECTION=evidence, updated September 1, 2012.
3. -www.bottomlinepublications.com, Health & Healing, Daily Health News, October 11, 2012, Article: Drink This to Sleep Soundly, Editor: Tamara Eberlein; Source: Lourdes Franco, graduate researcher, laboratory of chrononutrition, Department of Physiology, University of Extremadura, Badajoz, Spain. Study published in PLoS ONE. Additional sources: Keith Lemcke, Vice President, Siebel Institute of Technology, and World Brewing Academy, both in Chicago.

Chapter 12

1. www.ezinearticles.com/?The-benefits-of-eating-six-small-meals&id=1420774, article: The Benefits of Eating Six Small

Meals, by; The Fuzz, dated August 18, 2008. Article source: http://EzinArticles.com/?expert=teh_fuzz.

www.livestrong.com/Article/200706-how-to-eat-five-small-meals-a-day-to-lose-weight/, Article: How To Eat Five Small Meals a Day To Lose Weight, dated August 16, 2013, by; Dave Samuels. References: mayoclinic.com; Counting Calories: Get Back To Weight Loss Basics Asian Food Information Centre: Grazing For Weight Loss, mayoclinic.com: Why does Eating Breakfast Help Control Weight.

2. www.Heart.org, type in search bar, "Benefits of Apples", for numerous public articles.

www.healthdiaries.com/eatthis/10-health-benefits-of-apples.html, Article; 10 Health Benefits of Apples, published October 25, 2007, no author listed.

www.huffingtonpost.com, type in 'health benefits of apples' in search bar. Numerous articles posted, i.e., September 17, 2011, by: Kerri-Ann Jennings, Associate Nutrition Editor for Eating Well Magazine.

www.besthealthmag.ca/eat-well/nutrition/15-health-benefits-of-eating-apples, Article/slide show not dated and no author listed.

www.flatstomachblog.com/2008/12/09/30-benefits-eating-apple-day, Article: 30 Benefits of Eating an Apple a Day; Posted by: Jessica Oxford on December 9, 2008.

3. www.colgate.com, current information on gum disease.

www.medicinenet.com, numerous research articles on gum disease.

www.nidcr.nih.gov/OralHealth/Topics/GumDiseases/PeriodontalGumDisease.htm, National Institute of Dental and Craniofacial Research, numerous articles and information on gum disease.

www.perio.org/consumer/types-gum-disease.html, Website for the American Academy of Periodontology, research and information on gum disease.

www.bottomlinepublications.com/content/article/health-a-healing/you-can-have-a-much-younger-body-and-mind, Bottom Line Health, editor: Rebecca Shannonhouse, article: You Can Have a Much Younger Body And Mind, dated July 1, 2013. Source: Mike Moreno, MD, who is on the board of the San Diego Chapter of the American Academy of Family Physicians. He is also author of 'The 17 Day Plan To Stop Aging'.

4. www.bottomlinepublications.com/content/article/diet-a-exercise/5-cups-of-coffee-a-day-can-be-good-for-you, article; 5 Cups Of Coffee A Day Can Be good For You, by: Editor, Karen Larson, dated January 1, 2012.

www.hsph.harvard.edu/news/hsph-in-the-news/coffee-appears-to-protect-against-heart-failure-skin-cancer-2/, Harvard School of Public Health article: Coffee Appears To Protect Against Heart Failure, Skin Cancer. Published July 2, 2012.

www.hsph.harvard.edu/hpfs/hpfspublications.htm, click on 2013 Newsletter, article from the Health Professionals Follow-Up Study Newsletter for Winter 2013, page 2.

www.hsph.harvard.edu/nutritionsource/coffee/, Harvard School of Public Health article: Ask The Expert; Coffee and Health, by :Rob Van Dam, assistant professor in the Department of Nutrition, Harvard School of Public Health.

www.bottomlinepublications.com/content/article/diet-a-exercise/coffee-drinkers-live-longer, article; Coffee Drinkers Live Longer, by, editor Tamara Eberlein, published August 7, 2012.

www.theweek.com/article/index/244468/7-purported-health-benefits-of-drinking-coffee#, article: 9 Purpoted Heal Benefits of Drinking Coffee, Java May Make you Healthier, Smarter and Slimmer-But Not If You Drown It With Sugar And Cream, by: Chris Gayomali, science and technology editor for TheWeek.com, published May 21, 2013; Updated July 25, 2013.

www.bottomlinepublications.com/content/article/health-a-healing/drink-coffee-eat-chocolate, website article published May 1, 2008.

www.hsph.harvard.edu/news/multimedia-article/benefits/, article: Coffee & Health, by Harvard School of Public Health.

www.bottomlinepublications.com/content/article/diet-a-exercise/a-cup-of-decaf-may-prevent-memory-loss, article; A Cup of Decaf May Prevent Memory Loss, by editor: Tamara Eberlein, published June 5, 2012.

www.hsph.harvard.edu/news/press-releases/prostate-cancer-coffee-mucci-wilson, article by: Harvard School of Public Health, dated May 17, 2011: Coffee May Reduce Risk of Lethal Prostate Cancer in Men.

www.bottomlinepublications.com/content/drafts/the-real-scoop-on-coffee-and-caffeine, article: The Real Scoop on Coffee and Caffeine, published May 1, 2008, Bottom Line Women's Health interviewed Joann E. Manson, MD, DrPH, a professor of medicine and women's health at Harvard Medical School and chief of the division of preventative medicine at Brigham and Women's Hospital, both in Boston.

www.bottomlinepublications.com/content/article/diet-a-exercise/how-coffee-makes-you-happier-and-healthier, article: How Coffee Makes You Happier and Healthier, published September 5, 2013, by Daily Health News editor, Tamara Ebertein. Sources: Neal D. Freedman, PhD, MPH, cancer prevention fellow, division of cancer epidemiology and genetics, National Cancer institute, Rockville, Maryland. Frank B. Hu, MD, PhD, an epidemiologist, nutritional specialist and professor of medicine at Harvard Medical School of Public Health, both in Boston.

www.wikipedia.org/wiki/list of coffee varieties, basic information on coffee bean varieties, last updated August 18, 2013.

www.talkaboutcoffee.com/coffee beans.html, article: Coffee Beans-The Many Varieties of The Coffee Plant. No author or published date reflected.

5.   www.livestrong.com/article/324328-what-is-raw-unfiltered-honey, article: What Is Raw Unfiltered honey? By: Bridget Coila, published December 3, 2010.

www.benefits-of-honey.com/raw-honey.html, website article, no author or date.

www.vauhl.com/the-many-benefits-of-raw-unfiltered-honey, website article dated September 2, 2013, no author cited.

www.bottomlinepublications.com/content/article/diet-a-exercise/why-ugly-honey-is-better, article, Why Ugly Honey Is Better, published August 23, 2012, no author cited.

Chapter 18

1.   www.bottomlinepublications.com/content/article/health-a-healing/water-helps-your-brain, Article: Water Helps your Brain, by: Bottom Line Secrets, published January 15, 2013. Source: Daniel G. Amen, MD and Tana Amen, RN, BSN. Dr. Amen is a brain-imaging specialist and assistant clinical professor of psychiatry and human behavior at the University of California, Irvine, School of Medicine. Tana Amen is a nutritional expert and neurological intensive care nurse. Dr. Amen is author of: Use Your Brain To Change Your Age.

www.mangosteen-natural-remedies.com/benefits-of-drinking-water.html, article: Top 11 Benefits of Drinking Water and How. Undated/no author.

www.webmd.com/diet/features/6-reasons-to-drink-water, article: 6 Reasons to Drink Water, by: Kathleen M. Zelman, MPH, RD, LD. Reviewed by Louise Chang, MD. Published/Reviewed May 8, 2008.

www.bottomlinepublications.com/content/health-a-healing/the-simplest-prescription-of-all, Article: The Simplest Prescription of All, published by: Bottom Line Secrets. Published april 1, 2012. Source: Jamison Staarbuck, ND, is a Naturopathic physician, president of the American Association of Naturopathic Physicians and a contributing editor to The Alternative Advisor: The Complete Guide To Natural Therapies & Alternative Treatments.

www.bottomlinepublications.com/content/article/health-a-healing/drink-water-to-prevent-kidney-stones, Article: Drink Water To Prevent Kidney Stones, published January 15, 2009 by Bottom Line Secrets. Source: Bryan N. Becker, MD, professor of medicine, physician-in-chief and vice chair of the department of medicine and head of the nephrology section at the University of Wisconsin School of Medicine and Public Health, Madison, WI.

Chapter 20

1. www.bottomlinepublications.com, type in search bar, 'sleep deprivation' for numerous articles, i.e., on Lack of Sleep Increases Breast Cancer Recurrence Risk. Published on February 7, 2013 in Healthy Woman from Bottom Line. Source: Cheryl L. Thompson, PhD, is an assistant professor in the Department of Family Medicine Research and the Department of Epidemiology and Biostatistics at Case Western Reserve University School of Medicine in Cleveland. www.empowerHer.com/sleep-deprivation, article: Dangers of Sleep Deprivation, by Diberique Konig, published January 9, 2013.

www.webmd.com/sleep-disorders, article: Chronic Sleep Deprivation May Harm Health, by Michael J. Breus, PhD, published March 15, 2006.

2. www.OverDriveOnLine.com, article: Team Driving, published August, 2013, page 24.

Chapter 21

1. Al Sears, MD, www.alsearsMD.com, Article, Boost Oxygen Delivery To Your Cells By As Much As 2,000% In Just Minutes A day; Al Sears MD, Power For Healthy Living.
    www.oxygen4cells.com, Dr. Otto Warburg cancer research.
    www.stopcancer.com/ottolecture.htm, History of Dr. Otto Warburg.
    www.onepowerfulword.com/2010/10/18-benefits-of-deep-breathing-and-how.html, article: 18 Benefits of Deep Breathing and How to Breathe Deeply, by: Ash Srivastava, published in October, 2010.
    www.ehow.com/about_7227981_benefits-deep-breathing.html, article: Benefits of Deep Breathing, by: Meredith Gardner.
    www.breathing.com/articles/benefits.htm, article: Health Benefits of Optimal Breathing, by Michael G. White.
    www.womentowomen.com/fatigueandstress/deepbreathing.aspx, article: Fatigue & Insomnia, Deep Breathing—The Truly Essential Exercise, by: Marcelle Pick, OB/GYN NP. Article last updated April 20, 2011.

Chapter 24

1. American Trucking Association, on-line article; Truck Load and LTL Driver Turnover Rises in First Quarter of 2013, dated July 11, 2013.
    www.thecitywire.com/node/23969, article; Truck Driver Shortage Worsens, submitted by the city wire staff on 9/13/2012, story by Kim Souza.
    www.truckline.com/article.aspx?uid=d80ca14f-8656-408d-a34f-6b7c60ed0dce, article; Trucking Industry Has Current Shortage of 20,000 Drivers May Jump to 111,000 by 2014, dated 5/25/2005.
    www.npr.org/2013/09/02/216427414/truckers-shortage-worsens-as-energy-sector-booms, article: Trucker Shortage Worsens As Energy Sector Booms, by Andrew Schneider and Marilyn Geewax, dated 9/2/2013.

RESOURCES

www.schneider.com, the break-in company I started to work for. Good Company.

www.stevenstransport.com, another good company.

www.meltontruck.com, good nationwide flatbed trucking company.

www.safeway.com, look at bottom of web page under 'company information/careers'.

www.everytruckjob.com, appears to be a good source of available trucking jobs.

www.thetruckersreport.com, source for trucking industry news and articles.

www.richtruckdriver.com, this web site has some good information for the new driver.

www.overdriveOnline.com, The FREE on line version a trucking industry magazine.

www.Hotels4Truckers.com, This is an on-line directory hotels that are truck parking friendly.

www.catscale.com, and www.weighmytruck.com. In June of 2013 Cats Scale will be offering a smart phone application that will allow you to pull up to a Cat Scale, get weighed and pay for it with paypal, all without ever leaving your truck.

http://www.fmcsa.dot.gov, The Federal Motor Carriers Administration.

http://www.dot.gov, U.S. Department of Transportation.

http://mcsac.fmcsa.dot.gov, Motor Carrier Safety Advisory Committee.

http://safer.fmcsa.dot.gov/CompanySnapshot.ASPX, Carrier ratings.

http://csa.fmcsa.dot.gov/yourrole/drivers.aspx, You can find the Safety Measurement Severity (SMS)points for all violations.

http://nrcme.fmcsa.dot.gov, National registry of certified medical examiners.

www.aamva.org/cdl-program, American Association of Motor Vehicle Administrators. To obtain information on state medical certification requirements.

www.fmcsa.dot.gov/about/news/news-releases/currentpress.aspx, Stay current with what is happening by visiting this FMCSA news web site.

www.distraction.gov, click on tab at top labeled 'Faces'.
www.youtube.com, type in search bar, 'Faces of Distraction'.
www.truckline.com, Commercial truck driver web site.
www.drivebigtrucks.com, another website for trucking industry news.
www.RelianceProducts.com, Company web site for ordering portable toilet, Luggable Loo.
www.earthing.com, Company that has taken advantage of some new health information about the source of inflammation in the body and how to mitigate that inflammation to help live a healthier life and with less pain.

Below is a partial list of a few trucking companies that have less than truckload (LTL) type jobs that you may look into after you have had the minimum amount of experience they require. These LTL companies offer a variety of different positions including Pick up and deliver drivers, extra drivers, dedicated drivers and hub drivers. Each company may have different qualifications, so contact each one to determine what jobs are available and where.

I recommend calling after you have at least 6 months experience, just to start a dialogue with each company so you can start to eliminate those that don't appeal to you. By the time you get the one year experience, you should have a narrowed the selection down to one to three companies that are interested in hiring you for one of these 'better' trucking jobs. This list is not complete, in that there may be other companies in your area as well, so do some more research.

1) ABF Freight Systems, www.abfs.com, www.abf.jobs.
2) Central Freight, www.centralfreight.com, 800-299-1099.
3) Con-Way, www.true2blue.com.
4) Estes Express Lines, www.estes-express.com, 1-877-957-4378.
5) FedEx, www.Fedex.com/gb/careers,
6) GI Trucking, www.gi-trucking.com, 408-286-3894.
7) J.B. Hunt, www.jbhunt.com.
8) Melton Trucking, www.meltontruck.com,
9) Milan Express, www.milanexpress.com, 800-231-7303.
10) New England Motor Freight, www.nemf.com, 908-965-0100.
11) New Penn Motor Express, www.newpenn.com, 718-366-7590.
12) Old Dominion Freight Lines, www.odfl.com, 800-775-9836.
13) PJAX Freight Systems, http://indeed.com/cmp/pjax-freight-systems, 502-772-1942.

14) Roadway Express, www.roadwayexpress.jobhat.com, 800-249-9730.

15) R + L Carriers, www.rlcarriers.com, 800-543-5589.

16) Saia, www.saiasecure.com/employment, 800-765-7242.

17) Schneider National, www.schneider.com,

18) Southeastern Freight Lines, www.sefl.com, 803-794-7300.

19) Stevens Transport, www.stevenstransport.com,

20) UPS, https://upsjobs.managehr.com

21) USF Holland / USF Reddaway, www.reddawayregional.com, 888-420-8960.

22) YellowTransportation, www.yrcw.com/careers, 866-378-4935.

23) Vitran Express (sister company of PJAX Freight Systems), www.vitran.com, 412-453-4922.

GLOSSARY TO TERMS

Every occupation has its own language. The trucking industry is no different. All the trucking terms I have used in this book are defined below.

BASIC—(Behavior Analysis and Safety Improvement Categories) Data from roadside inspections, safety based violations and State reported crashes are used to 'score' carriers and drivers.

Break-In-Company—Any trucking company that hires new, inexperienced drivers, fresh out of school.

Bunk—The rear sleeping and living area in the back of a large truck, behind the cab where the driver and passenger sit. DOT refers this as the 'sleeper berth', since this is the area of the truck where you sleep.

Cab—The front area of the truck that seats the driver and passenger. Not all cabs have sleeper berths. Those trucks used primarily for short delivery purposes do not have sleeper berths and are referred to as day cabs.

CDL College—Commercial Drivers License School, 14800 Smith Road, CO. 80011, (303)367-1030. www.cdlcollege.com.

CMV—Commercial Motor Vehicle.

Company Padlock-The padlock the company provides to apply to the trailer doors of a full trailer to help secure the load from theft. Also referred to as a War-Lock. (Chapter 4)

CSA—(Compliance, Safety and Accountability) Measures the on-road safety performance of carriers and drivers.

Deadhead—Anytime you are pulling an empty trailer.

D.O.T.—Department of Transportation.

Drive Axel/Tires—These are the rear tires on the truck. You have two axels with 4 tires on each axel. Usually you only have one axel driving the truck, but you have the ability to lock in the 2nd axel when you need the extra traction.

Drivers Daily Log—A paper and/or electronic means of documenting the activities of all CMV drivers. (Chapter 5)

Drivers Number—a six digit number, which starts with a '0', that identifies a specific driver and used for a variety of purpose.(Chapter 5)

Drop and Hook—This refers to the action of dropping a trailer, either empty or full, depending on your assignment, at a shipper's facility and then hooking up to a different trailer, again, either empty or full depending on your assignment. (Chapter 4)

Empty Trailer—A trailer that does not contain any product. It is completely empty. (Chapter 4)

ETA—Estimated time of arrival. (Chapter 6)

Eleven Hour driving Limit (11 hour)—A commercial truck driver may drive a maximum of 11 hours after 10 consecutive hours off duty. (Chapter 5)

Fifth Wheel—The fifth wheel is that large semi-round 3" thick platform of steel with the hole in the center located at the rear of the truck, which connects the tractor and the trailer together. There are two plates involved. The lower plate or the platform mounted on the rear of the tractor (with the hole in the center) and the upper part of the fifth wheel is the 1" thick steel plate, also called an apron, that is built into the front of the trailer with the king pin welded to it. The truck's steel platform slides under the steel apron of the trailer, lifting the trailer slightly allowing the king pin to slid into the hole in the trucks platform and lock into place.

Floating Gears-When you change gears in a truck without using the clutch. If the speed of the truck and the RPM of the engine are just right, you can move in and out of gears without using the clutch. (Chapter 4)

Fourteen Hour Limit (14 hour)—A commercial truck driver may not drive beyond the 14th consecutive hour after coming on duty, following 10 consecutive hours off duty. Off Duty time does not extend the 14 hour period. (Chapter 5)

Gaskets—These are rubber grommets that fit inside the glad hands to prevent air from leaking out. (Chapter 7)

Glad Hands—These are the steel devices at the end of the air hoses that allow them to quickly connect and disconnect the air lines between the tractor and the trailer. These air hoses are located outside the rear of the truck cab and on the front of the trailer. (Chapter 7)

HOS (Hours of Service)—As a commercial driver, you are limited to 11 hours of actual driving time, 14 hours of 'On Duty' status (you have 14 hours to get in a maximum of 11 hours of driving), and depending on which gauge your company chooses for you, as soon as you reach a cumulative 60 hours in 7 days or 70 hours in 8 days, you are required to stop and take a 34 hour reset or break. (Chapter 5)

HOS Violation—Any time the 11 hour, 14 hour or 60 or70 hour rules are exceeded. (Chapter 5)

Independent Contractor (IC)—This is a driver who owns one or more trucks.

JackKnife—When the tractor is placed at a severe angle to the trailer. This term is used to refer to a type of accident when either the truck or trailer loses traction and starts to slide independently. This often results in an accident where the truck and trailer end up crushed up against each other at a sharp angle.

King Pin—This is the large steel pin that sticks out from under the steel apron at the front of the trailer. The king pin slides into the hole in the lower fifth wheel located behind the truck and is the actual part that holds the truck and trailer together.

Landing Gear—The landing gear holds up and supports the front of the trailer when unhooked from the tractor. Sometimes referred to as the 'dollies'.

Live Load-When you are hooked up to an empty trailer, back it into a dock, and have it loaded with product while you wait. (Chapter 4)

Log Falsification—When supporting documents, such as toll receipts, copies of roadside inspections, fuel receipts, etc., are compared to the log (paper or electronic) and there is a discrepancy of either location and/or duty status. (Chapter 5)

Motor Carrier—The legal terminology used to refer to any Trucking Company. (Chapter 5)

Motor Carriers' Road Atlas—A type of road atlas used by professional drivers.

NAT—Next available time. (Chapter 6)

Off Duty—The status of a driver when he is sleeping, eating a meal, spending time at home, or is not engaged in any activity that would be considered having some responsibilities for the carrier. (Chapter 5)

On Duty—The status of a driver when is either driving or engaged in responsibilities for the carrier. (Chapter 5)

Owner Operator—A person who owns the tractor they are driving. Some owners also own their own trailer.

Out of Service Order—When you pull into an inspection station of any kind or are pulled over and a violation is found that requires the defect or violation to be fixed prior to being released, an out of service order is issued. This prevents the truck from being moved until the violation is taken care of.

Pre-Loaded Trailer-When you drop an empty trailer at any warehouse or manufacturer, they will use their own 'yard dog' to pick the trailer up, back it into the dock, and load their product into that trailer. They will then close up the trailer doors, apply a seal and move the trailer to another area. They then call the company that owns the trailer and advise them they have a full trailer that needs to go to Dallas, or Los Angeles or wherever. If you happen to be unloading or dropping a trailer in the area, you may get the assignment to pick that trailer up and take it to its destination. (Chapter 4)

Pre-Trip Inspection—This type of inspection is done at the beginning of every trip to make sure there your tractor and trailer are in good operating condition. You would also do this type of inspection anytime you pick up a new trailer.

Post-Trip Inspection—This type of inspection is done at the end of every of each day and also every time you drop a trailer, since that is the end of the trip for that particular trailer. Your looking for anything that might have malfunctioned during the trip and since the last inspection.

Power Divider—This device divides the power equally between both drive axels and locks them together. You should use the power divider any time you need additional traction.

Qualcomm—This is the name of the company in San Diego, CA., that developed and owns the communication devices found in the truck cabs of several trucking companies.

Shipping Paper—This is the invoice type paper you will receive from the shipper when you pick up your load. The shipping paper will indicate what the product is, the quantity and its destination, among other things.

Sixty/Seventy (60/70) Hour On Duty Limit—A commercial truck driver may not drive after 60/70 hours of on duty status in 7/8 consecutive days. A driver may restart a 7/8 consecutive day period after taking 34 or more consecutive hours off duty. (Chapter 5)

Skip Shifting-This is when, while up shifting, you skip a gear. For example, you go from 2nd gear to 4th gear, and then 6th gear. This technique gets the truck up to speed faster and saves fuel. (Chapter 4)

Sleeper Berth—Commercial drivers using the sleeper berth provision must take at least 8 consecutive hours in the sleeper berth, plus a separate 2 consecutive hours either in the sleeper berth, off duty or any combinations of the two. (Chapter 5)

Steer Axel/Tires—The front axle and tires of the truck.

Tandem Axle—The axles and tires at the back of the trailer. These axels have the ability to slide from front to back and back to front, approximately ten feet. You pull the locking pins out and slide the wheels under the trailer in order to help balance your load and to comply with the various bridge laws.

TIV (Trailer Integrity Verification)—This is included in every Pre-Trip and Post-Trip inspection as well as enroute inspections. This inspection is designed to make sure no one has tampered with your trailer or has placed something on the truck that does not belong there.

TransFlo—The method of Faxing the Bill of Lading and Proof of Delivery to your company. The company must receive this proof of delivery before you can get paid.

War Lock-This is a lock provided by your employer to lock the trailer doors after you have picked up a loaded trailer or have had an empty trailer live loaded. This is designed to help secure the load from theft. (Chapter 4)

Workflow—This is a systematic system of issuing assignments/loads and the subsequent administration of said load from pick up to delivery.